SISTA POWER

DISCOVERING THE POWER OF COLLABORATIONS

BIDEMI MARK-MORDI

Verbatim Communications
Lagos, Nigeria

Published by Verbatim Communications Limited
Festival Suites, 5th Avenue A1 Close, Festac Town, Lagos.
Verbatimcommunications@yahoo.com
+234(0)8029056642

All scripture quotations, except otherwise stated, are taken from the Holy Bible, New King James Version. Copyright © 1979, 1980, 1982 by Thomas Nelson, Inc. All rights reserved.

ISBN 978-978-42000-7-3

Printed and Bound in Nigeria

*The bracelets represented on the cover image are courtesy Woman Act Now Inc. Please contact the publishers to get in touch with the Nigerian Chapter of the organisation.

DEDICATION

To Jesus, My Lord, Saviour and Redeemer; who gave me a second chance.

To Mark, my husband, brother, friend, partner and my most meaningful collaboration ever.

To my children; Kenechi, Dukia and Joshua; I can see the seeds of a great collaboration in you all when you play or work together. This is a God thing, I love you all.

Thank you.

CONTENTS

CONTENTS

ACKNOWLEDGMENT

It is impossible, really, to acknowledge everyone that I should on the pages of this book; however, I will try and hope that everyone else will understand my heart.

First, I want to celebrate my mother, friend and greatest fan of all time, Victoria Obarimike Adesunloye, your relentless pursuit of me ensured that the devil did not have his way in my life. I am grateful.

I cannot but say thank you to my husband Mark Mordi, for never telling me it cannot be done, thank you.

Remi, my Managing Editor and GPS sista, thank you for all the hard work you put into this.

Iboro Tonye-Edet, for buying into my vision and lending your skill and support, I am most grateful.

Charles Ibanga, you gave me one year of your life, and I will never forget the humility and zeal you brought even into the most mundane tasks. Thank you.

Audrey Joe-Ezigbo, for holding me accountable to this dream and the many ways in which you put me under scrutiny, I appreciate you.

The Sistahood; Ini Onuk, Enife Atobiloye, Inyang Sami-Orungbe, Nneka Nwobi and Audrey Joe-Ezigbo, you were the testees for this collaboration, in you I can testify that women can truly and really work and dream together. You are loved and appreciated.

For every staff of Verbatim Communications, past and present, thanks for enduring me and lending your life to my work, God bless you.

To my entire family, where will I be without you all? Thank you.

My Coach, Mentor, Friend and Sista, Coach Anna McCoy, your mark upon my life and dream is indelible. Thank you for bringing your dream to Africa, you are loved and appreciated.

And every woman and man who will pick up this book, it is now off my hands. The ball is in your court, my prayer is that you will find a way to bring your gifts to bear upon your relationships and collaborations and together fulfil destiny. It was indeed an honour bringing this to you. God bless you immensely.

Bidemi Mark-Mordi

FOREWORD

Coals stay hotter and brighter when clustered together. But separate one from the group, and it quickly grows cold and faint. So it is when one woman is left to her own way. The Apostle Peter suggests that God designed us to operate as living stones collected to form a spiritual temple (1Peter 2:5). Similarly, the Apostle Paul encourages us to act like the human body; many individual parts, each with their own function, working together to accomplish the dictates and desires of the Head, who is Christ (1Corinthians 12:12-31). We obviously can't do this alone. We are meant to collaborate!

During my sophomore year in high-school, I began playing basketball and I wasn't very skillful competitively. However, my sister, Sonya, was an all-star conference player, breaking records and upsetting teams with her double digit scores. I was so terrible; I was only used as her double when she would foul out of the game with only seconds left to play. I have always been an achiever and this humiliation was unacceptable for my personal best. After a disastrous effort that season, I said to Sonya, "look I need your help, because I have a goal to accomplish, I can't sit on that bench next season. I know I am not very good but I have some raw skills you can work with. Will you help me get on the starting lineup for next season?" She said, "Anna we can work together but you have to be serious and committed and we will do this. Are you willing? We will have to practice in the off-season before we practice other sports. After those practices, if you commit, I think you can do it." My sister and I created an indelible blueprint of supportive sisterhood in our hearts that no matter what we could do anything as long as we supported each other.

Thinking about my relationship with Sonya brings tears to my eyes because collaboration was the key. The two of us agreed upon a common goal and we achieved it. I started the first game of the season as a starting player and finished every game alongside my sister as we dominated the boards often sharing double digit scores and leading our team to an eighteen game winning streak. We became sista power on that court, supporting each other and our team to District and Area victories. We both were voted to our area wide all-star teams.

I really don't get the, "I don't usually relate to women," comments from other women. My life has been so enriched by the supportive relationships from women, old and young. Each time I hear this statement, my heart breaks for that woman. I can only imagine that she has never had the privilege of a sista-sista relationship where the culture of honour is its foundation and we win together.

Bidemi Mark-Mordi has captured the convincing essence of the necessity to collaborate with each other, sista to sista, heart to heart, dream to dream. Life, now and in the future, will always beckon women to arise and achieve their destiny. The challenges women face throughout the world will not change in a day, but like the faith required to move a mountain, one chip at a time is also the hopeful encouragement needed to midwife the dreams of one woman at a time.

Bidemi sent me an email expressing her desire to connect after reading my book, Woman Act Now. She was a bit nervous, she says, but her email was direct, approving and validating about our common interest. She was not given to much flattery or too many words; she just wanted to know if we could connect. I immediately responded with a similar posture being direct, approving and validating and informed her of my plans of visiting Lagos, Nigeria in seven months.

It didn't take long to recognize a few things about Bidemi that spoke volumes to me that she would become a rocking chair buddy in my life. She was serious about her relentless commitment to empowering women to achieve their God-given destiny. This root system of our shared passion would become the plumb-line and the measure of how deep our relationship could go. She is an executor, and a collaborator. Our commonalities along with our commitment to God created a three braided cord that would interweave our stories and purposes like a finely woven tapestry.

Her collaborative attitude is the spark of this book. It flows from her heart unbridled; it is the essence of a connection aimed at ensuring that all parties involved win. I want to encourage you to read Sistapower and if you are remotely guilty of thinking you can make it without your sisters at your side, get ready to be shifted. Enough of that lie persuading you to do it alone!

This book is about helping you make the connection, overcoming the status quo, arising to becoming your best while giving your best to others. You will learn how to recognize the importance of midwives and how to act as a midwife in the life of another. You will be convinced that you matter; your actions matter and your purpose must be fulfilled as your heart opens to receive and recognise the help that God sends your way.

Bidemi gives us countless biblical examples of the Master's collaborative doing among many familiar relationships, Mary and Elizabeth, Naomi and Ruth, Jonathan and David each teaching us the rules of engagement and the essentials required to be effective in these relationships to transform and reform our own life, family, community and possibly the world.

If you have found this book in your hand, whether gifted, purchased or found on a coffee table, I encourage you to keep turning the pages and open your heart to experience the power of becoming an exceptional woman who will accept the midwives in your life and learn how to become a sista who will undergird others with the power that resonates from within you.

Coach Anna McCoy
Founder, Woman Act Now
Texas, USA

INTRODUCTION

Dear reader, thank you for picking this book off the shelf, you must have a heart to impact and impart the lives of those whom you will come across. A lot of the decisions I have made in my life have been deliberate and calculating, some of them paid off and some didn't.

However, the two most important decisions I have had to make after accepting Jesus as my Lord and Saviour were definitely made for me by God Himself; and for both of them I am extremely grateful.

The first was the choice of the man I got to marry; it was all God and I am grateful He chose Mark for me. The second decision is going into Ministry as we know it. I didn't choose this path I can assure you, but I couldn't have made a better choice ever!

So this call has afforded me the opportunity to walk as closely as I am able to with God these years and it has been a life of learning, implementing, unlearning and relearning. In all these, God's faithfulness has been the reason why I wake up each day and determine to go on.

As one year gives way to another, I have learnt to go to God- the Source of life and all things- to get a blue print for what the new year holds and what I need to do to ensure that I remain in His will. This exercise has paid off tremendously. I have learnt to move into life in anticipation based on what I have heard Him say and follow through on the instructions to ensure their manifestation.

I always knew I was going to write books, but I never thought that my first book will have to do with collaborations, since I am pretty much someone who enjoys the ability to run alone and achieve things alone.

However, as the year 2010 came to an end and I went to God, as I will normally do, I heard that there was a new thing that God wanted to do. It was to begin to give voice to His daughters and bring them, as many as will listen to His voice and do His will, to a place of prominence and abundance. This was wonderful news to me, considering that I have always believed that women held a special place in God's heart and will play a vital role in God's move for a new season.

The subject matter of this book is what I have heard my

Father speak to me, and the more I studied this subject, the more it has become clear to me that I needed to share it with as many as will pick this book off the shelf and read to apply its principles for themselves.

This, for me, is a ride to another level of destiny fulfilment and as you take your place and knuckle down to learn and apply the principles, I look forward to the day when women from all over will share and make their gifts available to each other so that God's wonderful destiny for mankind will be fulfilled.

The Mandate

As I pressed into the Lord to ask what He will have me do in the year 2011, I heard Him declare that He has "now made plans to release an abundance to women to further His will and bring about change in the earth." This mandate sounded superficial to me at the beginning. It seemed that God wasn't saying anything that I had not heard before, so it didn't seem that there was a revelation in the words I heard. But I wanted to know more, so I started to ask more questions.

Like Mary I asked, "How will this be?" and I heard the response, "In coming together to fight battles, win wars and claim victory together!"

God gave me a sign; He promised that in a very short time - so I would recognize that it was He who was speaking - He was going to raise for me a group of women, who will make themselves available to work with me on my dreams and birth them together. It seemed like an impossible feat, but brethren, I have never seen a promise manifest as fast as this one had.

Each day I picked my Bible or meditated on Bible stories, every story started to unravel to reveal how much people achieved when they dreamed and birthed their dreams together.

The mandate for this book is a call for allegiance; it is a call for women all over to begin to recognize that God has called us individually, yes, but that He has also called us to connect with others so that the fullness of our destinies will begin.

Jochebed became pregnant with her son, Moses, during one of the most difficult times in the history of the Israelites. She was carrying a child of destiny no doubt, but it didn't look like this destiny was going to manifest if all that was going on with the Israelites at the time was to be considered.

The Pharaoh at the time had issued a decree that every male child born of the Israelites in Egypt should be killed. And so Jochebed recognized that it was almost impossible to see this destiny birthed let alone nurtured to fulfilment! But God had a plan. He had set in motion a series of events involving three other most unlikely women to ensure that the baby, who was put in a basket on the River Nile, will make it into destiny!

It all began with the midwives. Even though the decree had been issued, somehow they couldn't bring themselves to report the births of male children in Israel. Their excuse was that the Hebrew women had their children fast! And the Bible records that God blessed them for it.

Then the baby's teenage sister, Miriam! Who would have thought that a girl that young would know what to do at such a perilous time? But Miriam was put there by God to not only watch over the baby and the basket, but also to buy him more nurture time. Miriam somehow recognized that she was in an opportune time, and even though she was young and inexperienced, she used her voice. All she suggested to Pharaoh's daughter was to get a nurse for the baby. The Bible doesn't expressly say so, but I think that someone must have been praying; maybe Jochebed, maybe even Miriam! Anyhow, this simple suggestion was enough to convince Pharaoh's daughter.

By speaking up, Miriam bought the child three years in which he was looked after by his own mother. It was also enough time for him to be taught all that the Jewish race stood for, and who their God was! Three years was all Miriam could do, but it was also all that Moses required for the book of the law to be ingrained and engraved in his heart for the future!

What about the woman who saw the baby and fell in love with him instantly? She was not even Jewish and she wasn't unaware that there was a decree for all male children born by the Jews under three years of age to be killed. But she did fall in love with the child and nothing was going to let her give him up to be killed. What love was this? Who put that measure of love in her heart?

All these because the destiny of a deliverer for the children of Israel was in this child! Where else could God hide His ace if not directly inside the palace of the enemy and who better to look after him, but the enemy's closest relative?

Under this mandate, I must quickly tell you that there is utmost need to be tuned into the directives and commands of the Most High God. What we are talking about here has nothing to do with class, status or rank; it is all about God. Therefore we need to ensure that we are not swayed by outward appearances, but taking an essential look at our heart, we should determine what God would have us do.

Why Collaboration?

In answering this question, let us imagine for just a minute that when the Jewish women went into labour the Egyptian midwives sent for the palace guards, or that Miriam refused to stay by the edge of the water to watch her baby brother's basket float down the river. What if Pharaoh's daughter didn't come to the river that day and time for her bath? Or what if when she saw the baby she also sent for the palace guards?

Yes I know that God would still have been able to ensure that His purpose was fulfilled, but how would the story have ended for these women above? Just like that day when God needed a deliverer for His children, God still has great plans for the emancipation of mankind, and just as these women played a major role in bringing it to pass; you and I have a part to play.

The Bible puts it this way, "a threefold cord cannot be easily broken." What that means is that every venture takes more than one person's input and once we have enough people making their input the impact will be a lot more effective.

As regards what I can hear in God's heart, we have a need to collaborate for a different number of reasons. First being that the end is near and we are running out of time. What needs to be done to ensure the salvation and deliverance of many needs to be done fast.
Secondly, the final battle between the seed of the woman and the Anti-Christ is on. Literally, there is a battle raging between the kingdom of God and that of the devil and the earlier we all contributed our quota the easier the victory. There is something about the woman and her womb that the devil hates

so much, and we cannot afford to be ignorant and allow him keep us divided; because the more the division, the easier it is for him to prevail.

Finally, women were called to become helpmeets for the men, and rebuilders of destinies to ensure that God's mandate comes to pass. However, because we live in a fallen world, and the order as ordained by God has been disrupted and in some cases usurped, we find that men are no longer living as the rulers and priests of the their homes; the women are taking over. Collaboration is therefore, another way through which God wants to restore the order as laid down from the beginning so that victory can be ensured.

The mandate of this message is therefore to sensitize and encourage the women to form allegiances that will bring about a fulfilment of each individual destiny vis-à-vis God's order. Women need to return to the place where children were jointly raised, communities were built together and everyone contributed whatever they had been endowed with.

The mandate of this message is to encourage women to come out globally and be there for each other and in the process restore God's will. If you are conversant with world happenings and politics, you will find that in my country, Nigeria, and even in the Middle-east, we are beginning to see women come together a lot more to insist that change comes in their nations.

In the business world, a lot more women are stepping up to the plate, setting up businesses in what used to hitherto be 'men only' territories; and they are doing well. Most importantly, even the men are beginning to recognize that women have a great deal to contribute, so recourse is being made to women a lot more frequently than in the past.

The mandate therefore is not selfish; it is about God's big picture and how we can change the status quo especially where it is so glaring that things have gone wrong. This mandate is about empowering the girl child to recognize the power she carries and ensuring that her dreams are birthed. This mandate is about what we can do and not what we have been told we can do.

So settle in as we move into the basics and the workings of collaborations. I do know that if you embrace these principles and run with them, there is no telling how far you can go. In the end, whether you collaborate to build a business, a home or raise a child, always remember that God is interested in how it all unfolds. Welcome again, and God bless you.

1 AND GOD BEGINS A NEW THING

When I got commissioned into doing this work, I received the scripture Jeremiah 31:22b "…for behold the LORD hath created a new thing in the earth. A woman shall encompass a man." Another version says, "…I have created something new and different, as different as a woman protecting a man." (Good News Bible).

This scripture has remained with me these past ten years and every time I take time to meditate on it, I see fresh angles from which it still speaks to me. The truth of the matter is there is a new move, and women are in the fore front. I keep telling people that this is not about usurping the position of the man especially in the homes. It is a mandate given by God to the woman to ensure and guard jealously the order that He, God, Himself has

When I got commissioned into doing this work, I received the scripture Jeremiah 31:22b "…for behold the LORD hath created a new thing in the earth. A woman shall encompass a man."

ordained for the systems of the world and all that they stand for. I took time to study this scripture and I found out that the word 'encompass' has about nine synonyms that were relevant to the context of the scripture. They are:

1. Protect, which had as offshoots words like Shield/Circle/Intercede
2. Overpower, with words like Influence/Teach/Lead as its offshoots.
3. Nurse which also had words like Nurture/Love/Care.

I also discovered that the Hebrew word for man as used in Jeremiah 31:22b, was not about man as the male gender, but a word for mankind, which means that we (both male and female) have been called to encompass the entire world.

If we were to use the above synonyms contextually, Jeremiah 31:22b, will read something like this "… the Lord has begun a new thing, the woman will protect, intercede for, teach, nurture, love and care for humanity just as the father does."

If this is a new thing, it therefore means that the old order will be changed or altered. Every time a new thing is born, the old is replaced, and if God wants us women to encompass the world, then it must mean that something is lacking in the order of things as it were.

"Now the Lord God said, it is not good (sufficient, satisfactory) that the man should be alone; I will make him a help meet (suitable, adapted, complimentary) for him" Genesis 2:18. The spiritual positioning of the woman therefore is about helping in every ramification of the word!

Mary Jean Pigeon in her book *"Woman: Purpose, Position, and Power"* states *"the power God has given the woman to motivate a man through her image is meant to achieve a divine purpose. As the man watches the woman, she is able to influence him into spiritual growth and to motivate him toward spiritual purity..."* She goes on to make the following observation, *"...if God created woman for a specific purpose, then the most powerful place she can be is in a position to accomplish that purpose."*

I am of the opinion that this positioning by God does not end in the homes. There is usually a ripple effect when a man is connected to a woman who compliments and completes him, to all other relationships the man may be involved in, especially in work and business. This goes on to affect society and in the end the

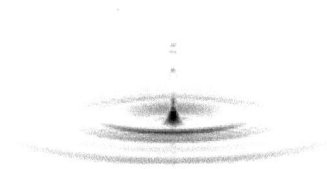

....there is usually a ripple effect when a man is connected to a woman who compliments and completes him, to all other relationships the man may be involved in, especially in work and business.

world is a better place. A typical example is the virtuous woman in the book of *Proverbs 31:10-31*.

A careful study of this woman goes a long way to show us what God expects from us women. We have been called to be a blessing not just to our husbands but also to members of our family and by extension to our community.

A virtuous woman exhibits these traits not just at home but also at work. In whatever position she finds herself, she displays integrity, she is hard working, industrious, has the welfare of her colleagues in mind and most of all contributes positively to the growth of her place of work.

We have been called to be industrious, hard working, kind and generous to the needy. When we fulfil this mandate, believe me not only will we be blessed by God, we will also be recognized as change agents and productive members of our society.

Even so, the mandate right now is that rather than try to do it all alone, we need to connect and join forces as God intended so we can bring about the change we so desire. The bible puts it this way *"And five of you shall chase an hundred, and an hundred of you shall put ten thousand to flight."*[2]Imagine what will happen if a thousand of us come together for the same cause. *A threefold cord is not easily broken- (See Leviticus 26:8 and*

Ecclesiastes 4:12). When we collaborate at home, at work or in our neighbourhood we become a strong force that cannot be resisted.

In this new thing that God is set to do with women, the three core areas that will be affected are our homes, work places and the society at large. Before civilization, women knew how to collaborate in raising their children. They looked out for each other, there was a great sense of community and a lot of progress and advancement followed.

But that was until we started to erect fences. Even as we erected these physical fences, we unknowingly erected them in our hearts too. Parenting is for instance, one of the parts of our life where we are beginning to miss it! In my generation and generations before us, children were usually raised by the entire community.

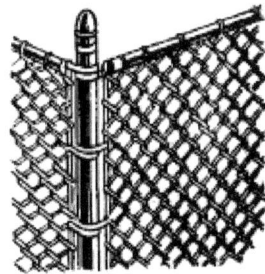

....as we erected these physical fences, we unknowingly erected them in our hearts too.

Mothers, aunts, grandmothers, even stepmothers worked together to ensure that the children all had value-added upbringing. But these days behind our walls and erected fences, we concentrate on our two, three or four children and insist that they do not mingle or relate with the children on the other side of the fence, because in our words, 'they are rough, wayward... etc'. What we forget however, is the fact that they may end up in the same schools, work on the same jobs, or may even end up falling in love with each other! When that happens, our perceived enemies make it into our homes, and we are taken by surprise!

As mothers we need to come together in one accord in ensuring that our children are brought up with the right ideologies. If we agree that covetousness is bad, then our children must have that drilled into them from an early age. If we know that gossip is wrong, then we stop it ourselves and discourage our children from engaging in such.

When children come to realize that their every move is being watched not only by their mothers but other women, then they will have no choice but to be of good behaviour at home, play or school. Bring up a child in the way he should go when he is old, he will not depart from it. This is the key to raising good citizens for our society. Our voices as mothers and women will be heard in the way our children live their lives in the bigger world.

On the other hand, when we get too concerned with our individual lives and immediate households only, we tend to forget that whatever we achieve behind our walls we will need to go out into the society and defend. The sad thing is that no matter how great our personal ideals and ideologies are, once we get into the society, our solo voices will be overwhelmed by all the other discordant ones.

Collaboration is not an easy principle especially if you consider the fact that human beings are different and that can pose a difficulty. But I feel God's heart saying that this is the only way to alter the status quo and bring about His divine order and will.

No one person has all that is required to get everything done, so there is a great need for us to relate with others. If we come together, breaking the barriers of occasional telephone calls and hellos, and create a presence in each other's lives, will it not be easier to bring about change?

What I am getting at is the fact that collaborating is meant to bring about change in every facet of the society, home, business, economy and so on. What this will achieve is that we will become accountable to each other, and we will all contribute our quota. More room is created for all to participate and each person brings in their gifts! There is more than enough room for everyone to participate in whatever role they fit in.

Changing the Status Quo

There is a story about five sisters who lived in a society that was culturally patriarchal; which means in that era they were pro-men. One of the issues that women contended with for example was that they were not allowed to receive an inheritance from their fathers. These five young women were the only children their father had. Unfortunately, they lost their father at an early age. A few years later, they had come of age and needed to declare their independence from relatives. Did their father leave anything in his will for them? No! Why, because they were daughters and not sons who would carry their father's name for generations to come. That was the rule of law then. But these sisters decided to make a move that changed history forever. I am talking about the story of the daughters of *Zelophehad* in *Numbers 27. Zelophehad* was one of those who did not make it out of the wilderness alive during the transition from Egypt to the Promised Land. It is recorded that he died of his own sins but was survived by five daughters *(Mahlah, Noah, Hoglah, Milcah, and Tirzah)*. These ladies had probably been worried over the fact that when they did get into the Promised Land, they may not have a place to stay and conduct their business, simply because they were women!

Even though the Bible does not give a detailed account of how they arrived at the decision to approach Moses to demand that they need not be punished for no fault of theirs, I believe it all began with a conversation, a suggestion, probably heated arguments and even disagreements but they finally did reach an agreement and with that united front they approached Moses and demanded that their share of their father's inheritance be handed over to them.

A number of things fall out of this story for me, and I will quickly point them out here.

Walking In Agreement

Imagine a scenario where two of the five sisters went to ask Moses for their inheritance, while the other three refused to give them support because they didn't believe in their demands? Imagine a different scenario where on getting to the camp, all five sisters started to quarrel over who gets what, even before Moses gave his verdict?

Good enough, none of these scenarios above played out. What the Bible records is that they approached Moses and the elders at the entrance of the camp of meeting. Together speaking with one voice! Of course you know that the fall out point for us here is that collaboration is enough to bring about change, we need to agree and speak with one voice! *Amos 3:3* summarily says that agreement is vital for any group of persons to walk or work together.

Something happened here in Nigeria and I want to draw another analogy from that. We held our elections in 2011 and leading up to it, the ruling party set a date to hold its primaries. Before then one very bold and courageous woman had indicated her intent to run, despite the fact that she had been told that the presidency of the nation was not for women. At the primaries she stood for herself and was the only one who voted for herself! Now the issue for me isn't whether she was ready to be a president or whether she had what it takes. The issue for me

AND GOD BEGINS A NEW THING

was she was making history as a woman and she was standing alone! Amongst the delegates that day, were other women, but not one of them even approached her after it all to pat her on the back to say well done. Or thank you for standing up for the women of Nigeria.

Instead we saw all kinds of cartoons and text messages sent mostly by other women, making jest of a woman who had mustered the courage to stand up for her convictions, even though she didn't have a plan or the resources to push through.

I looked into the future and said to myself in another ten years or even less, other women will be standing on the shoulders of what Dr. (Mrs.) Sarah Jubril has done, and all we can do is laugh at her?

The Zelophehad sisters, on their way to make their requests, must have been laughed at by other women. They would have told them that Jehovah Himself had given the directive that women should not get inheritances and that it was a futile thing they had set out to do, but it is clear that they didn't listen because they had each other to look to for support and encouragement.

Any wonder their story ended a little differently from Dr. (Mrs.) Jubril's?

The whole world may not be supportive and encouraging as long as you have your collaborator, then please keep moving.

Perfect Timing

There is something to be said about their timing! Did you notice their issue was the last one Moses dealt with before he was called home by God? They must have been praying! Their case was set and arranged on divine timing. Just like the opportune time for women to move closer to destiny is now, it was time for the daughters of Zelophehad, and they recognized the time and seized the opportunity. They went to Moses and even Moses couldn't decide on his own. His elders couldn't handle it either, so the Bible says Moses took the matter before God Himself!

And, wait for it, God ruled in their favour. God is a God of justice and this was His answer to Moses:

It was time for the daughters of Zelophehad, and they recognized the time and seized the opportunity.

"The daughters of Zelophehad are justified and speak correctly. You shall surely give them an inheritance among their father's brethren, and you shall cause their father's inheritance to pass to them" (Numbers 27:7).

And because the daughters came together, they received their request. But God didn't stop there; He went on to change the statute forever.

> *"And say to the Israelites, if a man dies and has no son, you shall cause his inheritance to pass to his daughter. If he has no daughter, you shall give his inheritance to his brethren; give his inheritance to his father's brethren..." Numbers 27:8-11.*

The big news about collaborations is that when we move at the appointed time, it brings about lasting change. Mindsets and traditions can be altered just because people got together to enforce their strengths, rights and beliefs. The nation of Israel changed forever, because of the daughters of Zelophehad's request. If they had approached Moses earlier than when they did who knows what would have happened? They could have been stoned to death for daring to speak against the laid down law. If they delayed, Moses could have been long gone and there'd be no one to listen to their case. They moved at the appointed time. You need discernment! Be observant and willing to make the move once you can tell the time is right.

Ecclesiastes says that everything has its time and season. In this case, the time to wait had passed; it was time to make that move. Even today, as you go out, listen to the news or just watch daily activities of life around you, you will notice that there is so much that needs to change to bring about the quality and standard of life that we are clamouring for. But if the saying that, little drops of water can make a great pool is true, imagine what will happen if we come together in agreement with our God-given mandate, recognizing that we are in an opportune time, and taking advantage of the time to bring about lasting change.

In my home country Nigeria there has been news about banks merging, to give better value, there have been talks about political parties forming alliances to ensure that change comes for the greater good of the people. When we collaborate we tend to lose autonomy of whatever we are working on, but the gains are a lot more far reaching even from God's perspective! This leads me to the final lesson we can draw from the daughters of Zelophehad.

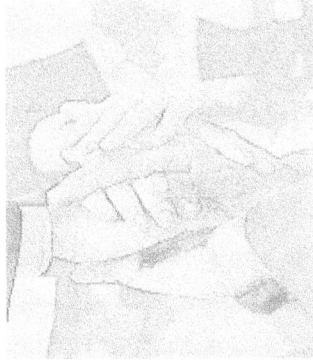

When we collaborate we tend to lose autonomy of whatever we are working on, but the gains are a lot more far reaching even from God's perspective!

For the Greater Good

Because these sisters stood up for what they believed in, even today, families in Israel are reaping the rewards. The value that can be created far exceeds the sacrifices that are made in the place of collaboration.

What qualities did these women possess? First I saw a group of women willing to stand for the right thing even though it wasn't the popular or accepted thing. This means an enlisting to go against the flow, swim against the tide and stand against the accepted norm. I saw a group of women willing to take on something apparently bigger than themselves. Approaching Moses with this request was taking on the entire Jewish race and culture as well as taking on the God of Israel Himself. They couldn't have been sure how it was all going to pan out, but they went on, I believe, by faith, and today generations are still reaping the reward.

I had the opportunity to teach this principle recently, and one of the things I said was that 'collaboration isn't about the individuals coming together as much as it is about the value that pooling resources and strengths together may be able to create.'

I was listening to an audio recording of a call in the John C.

Maxwell Coaching Class Founders Circle recently, and Scott Fay said that the world has evolved over the decades through some phases of civilisation, beginning from the Industrial age, to the Communication Age, to the Technological Age and now we are in the Association Age. For me, what this means is that this is a great time to get into collaborations for value.

The mandate is therefore for us to find points of dissatisfaction requiring change or improvement and search out like-minds so we can come together and begin to effect the required change and create eternal value. If the daughters of Zelophehad could do it, we certainly can do it too. Yes! We can!

Action Exercise

I) Based on what you have learnt in this chapter define collaboration in your own words.

ii) What change needs do you see in your immediate environment that you believe collaborations will help achieve?

iii) How do you think you can get people to collaborate with you? Write down two effective ways that come to mind.

iv) What is your purpose for collaborating and how do you intend to make these goals known to your fellow sistas?

2 DESTINY AND THE MIDWIFE

very great destiny is tied to a midwife, and I have had my own fair share of midwives. When I got married fifteen years ago, I had a mindset that my marriage was going to be really beautiful. We would never have an argument and we will live happily ever after. However, I had no clue how that was going to come to pass, so I kind of trusted in fate and chance. I thought if I was tough enough, or if I was a doormat enough this would become a reality.

When I got married fifteen years ago, I had a mindset that my marriage was going to be really beautiful. We would never have an argument and we will live happily ever after.

While I was looking forward to living happily ever after, the first thing I came to realise was that happily ever after was relatively dependent on what you were looking for! I also realised quickly that most people had no idea what happily ever after meant for anyone else but themselves, and to be honest most people's idea of happily ever after wasn't something I was willing to try out. Yes, I had good intentions, and Mark, my husband, had even better intentions but we just had no idea how to make the right decisions all the time - so we went searching for answers. One thing that was clear to both of us though, was that we wanted things to work and we were committed to making that happen. We defined what our happily ever after was meant to look like, and we set out to find answers and work at arriving there. Something amazing happened in the process.

Personally, more than the fact that I wanted my marriage to work, there was also the major issue of not knowing what I was on earth for. I had a job before I got married which I had to resign from just before the wedding. One of the reasons I quit was because of the mindset that once you get married all your problems would vanish!

Alas! It was not so. I found that marriage foisted on me more responsibilities than I had when I was single. I now had four parents to answer to and look after. I also quickly found out that no matter what my spouse earned, by the time we spread it round, we were spread too thin, and that also affected what we had perceived as our happily ever after. As you know the less money that is available within a marriage, the more pressure on the couple! Especially, if it is a young one as ours and the couple is yet to understand what their purpose is!

Like I said, despite all these, I had a bigger issue to contend with, and this was the fact that I had no idea what I was created for. I needed to find what to do to find fulfillment that wasn't tied to money or material possessions of any kind.

It was in the course of looking for something that will bring me joy and fulfillment that I started to read and study the Word. I meditated on what God had given to me by way of talents. I wanted to harness, improve on them, and put them to use.

I was blessed to be surrounded by a great group of people beginning from my Pastor, and Spiritual father, Pastor S.W. Ifie. Somehow, he saw in me gifts I didn't even know I possessed and the more I read, studied and meditated on what God had called me to do, the more Pastor Ifie provided me with the enabling environment to utilize my gifts. The more I used the gifts, the more it became clearer who I was called to be, and the more I walked in that call, the more fulfillment I got. At this point, it became easier to relate with my husband in abundance and in lack, because something else took the place of needing him to make me happy and fulfilled. Even though my life still

....the less money that is available within a marriage, the more pressure on the couple! Especially, if it is a young one as ours and the couple is yet to understand what their purpose

revolved around our idea of happily ever after, we started to realise that happily ever after for us, was contained in how much change we will birth for those around us. This revelation made it easier to face life even when things didn't quite go as we planned. It also gave us hope that as long as we remained in the place of our gifting and made ourselves available, we were bound to get better both financially and otherwise.

My destiny and the power to live it, was birthed by all kinds of midwives. There was the struggle to discover and define for myself what happily ever after was; this drove me to reading, asking questions and developing my gifts into strengths. There was also my Spiritual Father, who believed in me enough to give me an enabling environment to express my gift. There was my husband, who never doubted that I was able to do whatever I dreamed about and did not hesitate to tell me so, and there was the feeling of fulfillment that I got every time I lived on purpose.

I mentioned in the introduction to this book that Moses had a destiny to deliver the children of Israel from bondage, and that even though the destiny was his to fulfill, he needed help. God ensured that all the midwives of his destiny were in place. Some were his friends and family, some were strangers and there were those who were outright enemies, but with each relationship, Moses' place as a deliverer for the children of

Israel was strengthened and enhanced.

Let us look at some other midwives involved in the destinies of some important personalities in the Bible. First of all we'll look at Moses one more time: I mentioned midwives like Miriam, Pharoah's daughter and Jochebed, his biological mother. These women played important roles in ensuring that Moses stayed alive at a time when male children were sentenced to death before they were even born. But Moses' destiny was much more than being an adopted prince in the house of Pharaoh; God was just starting with him. The Bible records that:

"One day, after Moses was grown, it happened that he went out to his brethren and looked at their burdens; then he saw an Egyptian beating a Hebrew, one of Moses' brethren. He looked this way and that way and when he saw no one, he killed the Egyptian and hid him in the sand." Exodus 2:11-12.

Miriam, Pharoah's daughter and Jochebed, his biological mother. These women played important roles in ensuring that Moses stayed alive at a time when male children were sentenced to death

Why was that the first thing Moses witnessed that day? An Egyptian beating on a Hebrew slave! Yes I know, you may think it is just coincidence. But some wise person once said that coincidence is God performing a miracle and choosing to stay anonymous! So because Moses had need for further training and - this time it was a desert course - he just needed to witness this act against his brother. And why did he have to kill the guy? Couldn't separating them have sufficed? Because God wants to take you to another level, he is releasing some midwives for your destiny into your life. Some of them will be great and wonderful encouragers like my Pastor, and my husband, like Miriam and Pharaoh's daughter, but others will be the situations and circumstances such as the one Moses had to deal with on his first day out.

God puts midwives in our lives because He recognises our inability to submit to His will sometimes because of all the conflicting issues and circumstances we may encounter. Sometimes, midwives are put there to point us in the direction of what is important and sometimes the negative midwives are put there because God wants us to get creative and ask ourselves how we can step up and become more for Him!

Now the key is to realise that no matter what your midwife looks like, according to *Romans 8:28: "We are assured and know that (God being a partner in their labour) all things work together and are (fitting into a plan) for good to and for those who love God and are called according to (His) design and purpose."*

There is something that is greater than us all, and has the

capacity to ensure that our destinies come to pass whether the circumstance is palatable or not. Moses' story will not be complete without the help of the Egyptian who beat the Hebrew slave in his presence. And let's take it a step further, what would have happened had Moses controlled himself that day and walked away? My opinion is that Moses still had some growing up to do; even though the Bible says he was grown; so he had to do the indignant thing and kill the Egyptian. Automatically, the Prince becomes the fugitive and the next round of training begins.

Now, I recognise that most of our stories may not be as dramatic as Moses' but what we need to agree on is the fact that whatever our destinies are, we require a midwife or midwives to help us birth them. Another great destiny that needed midwives to help in its fulfillment was Joseph's. From a tender age, Joseph was destined to be a preserver for the children of Israel. His destiny came with position and status even though he was the last but one child in his family. The audacity to dream and see himself as someone his siblings will bow before nailed the coffin for him! How could he even imagine that he had a destiny that great? And like most families, not everyone could rejoice over the fact that Joseph was going somewhere great, and hard as they tried the only way out was to ensure his dream never came to pass! Though it didn't seem like it was God's will for him, it was part of the grand plan. For Joseph to fulfill his destiny some things just had to be right, even though it seemed wrong, and that included a trip to the pit, slavery and prison. Each time Joseph's condition got worse, it seemed that his dream was slipping away from him, but because the one that controls the affairs of men, had a thought pattern higher and grander than any man's, each of these circumstances were calculated to bring Joseph to the wealthy place!

Your life may be ridden with disappointments and depressing circumstances right now, but so were the lives of many great destinies that were birthed in the Bible. One thing that is common to most of them is the fact that they were faced with circumstances that, even though looked terrible, were the very factors that catapulted them into fulfilling their destinies.

Your life may be ridden with disappointments and depressing circumstances right now, but so were the lives of many great destinies

In the physical, no woman goes into the birthing or delivery room alone, doctors may not be available, but there is usually a midwife around to ensure that both mother and baby are fine. The midwife usually has an input and every wise woman listens to her, so that she is able to bring forth that which she has carried to term.

It follows therefore, that the midwife usually has some experience or information that the birth mother needs, so there is a need for them both to co-operate to ensure a safe delivery. The importance of listening to our midwives can therefore not be over emphasized.

I remember having midwives whose contributions could not be overlooked even though they were not physically present in my life. One of them is Pastor Rick Warren. As I write this book, I still haven't had the opportunity to meet him but through his book - The Purpose Driven Life - he made my quest for the fulfillment of destiny a whole lot easier. I say so because, of his past experiences and the discipline he had exerted to document them. His experiences helped me put things in perspective, to recognise what was important and what wasn't. So even though he doesn't know me in person, Rick Warren is one of those that came so I could be!

One of your midwives may be this book you hold in your hand, it may be another you are yet to purchase; it may be somebody's story that has inspired you to look beyond where you are and start to dream in colour. Whoever, or whatever they are, you have a responsibility to recognise them.

Recognising Your Midwife

One of the easiest ways to recognise a midwife is by what they bring into your life, and how what they bring aligns with God's word for your life. It may be a lot harder to recognise a midwife if you are still unsure of what your destiny is about. But even then, I can assure you that God will keep you and help you make some decisions you may not understand until later.

It is therefore important to know that our lives belong to God and He has a script written out, which may or may not play out the way we have imagined. I have trained myself to quickly ask, what is there to learn from this? This is because I am convinced God has a great interest in my life and so is constantly watching over me to ensure that I don't make useless mistakes. What this means is even when I make mistakes He takes them and uses them to bring out His glory.

So when I get into situations that could have been avoided and I try everything to avoid them and don't succeed, I submit and open my eyes to see what God has planned. If we will go back to the story of Moses for a minute, you will realise that he just picked himself up and ran as soon as he realised that what he had done was no longer a secret. And guess where he ran to? The land of Midian! Why Midian, because God recognised that the children of Israel who Moses was being called to lead, were more like the flock that he would learn to tend and care for in Midian.

It took Moses a long time to realise that all things were working together for his good. It took Joseph a while to realise that it wasn't the end of the road in slavery or in prison. And it

He just picked himself up and ran as soon as he realised that what he had done was no longer a secret.

may take you a while, before you realise the full implication of what you face and the role those around you have to play in bringing you to destiny. But the trick is this: "recognise your midwife."

Two Important Steps to recognising your midwife:

Be Open Minded

When it comes to recognising your midwife, keep an open mind. They may not come packaged the way you may prefer or anticipate. Sometimes, even the midwife may not understand the power they wield over your destiny, and they may never know, but it is your job to recognise them and key into what they have been ordained to deposit into your life.

The trappings and the fine manners of the palace did not suffice for the future when Moses would lead the children of Israel into the wilderness. How would Moses have coped except he had a firsthand taste of what the wilderness and tending herds entail? Moses needed the education, and killing an Egyptian opened the door for him to enroll in the school of wilderness training.

Submission

You need to submit to the training of the midwife. Except for what his mother had probably told him, about being a special child and one who would deliver the Israelites one day, Moses had no idea what his job description entailed. But he found himself in the home of Jethro, the Midianite, who happened to be his father in-law and the leadership training began in earnest. Moses had to learn to care for his herd, and love them tenderly, and these became some of his most enduring traits when he got back to his mission! Only someone who truly cared for and loved the Israelites would be able to lead them! If you remember God Himself described them as *"a stiff necked people."*

If Moses had not submitted to becoming a herdsman, he would not have been able to accept God's calling to deliver the children of Israel. Moses definitely needed the training to become a true shepherd. But even though Moses was in training, it seems to me he was the last to recognise what he had been called to do; at least the fullness of it. By the time he was ready God made the announcement via the burning bush! What other commissioning could he require after this?

My point is as long as you are carrying destiny, and I know you are, you will require midwives to take you through the birthing process. Some will be pleasant, others not so pleasant. Whatever it is you have to go through, however, recognise that there is a God who rules in the affairs of men, submit to the midwives and their different processes and you will be amazed at the magnitude of what you are called to do, and how you will turn out in the end. The idea is this; you are called to do something, and usually it is so much greater than you that you require a lot of help. Once your midwives begin to show up, do your best to submit to the process and accommodate them all, because your success may just be based on how much you allow yourself to learn from your midwife!

Moses submitted to the training in the wilderness; Joseph submitted to training in Potiphar's house and the prison; David submitted to King Saul's terrorism, and Daniel submitted to captivity in Babylon for years. But in all these, they came out great men of God.

You may have the opportunity to choose some midwives, others will be chosen for you! It really doesn't matter how they become your midwife, just know that in the end your destiny will be birthed and they have an input to make.

Above all if you recognise the sovereignty of God Almighty and how He is able to use us all for His glory, then it should make submitting to the process a lot more meaningful, if not easier.

In the end when you begin to birth your dreams and fulfill

destiny, you'll definitely become a midwife for another person and whatever you do, ensure that the deliveries you midwife are not still births.

Action Exercise

i) List at least three (3) people who have played the roles of midwives in your destiny? How did they do it?

ii) How did you recognise your midwives?

iii) Have you been a midwife to any destiny in the past or of late?

iv) How would you position yourself to be recognised as a midwife?

3
MAKING THE LIFE CONNECTION: FINDING YOUR KIND

About eleven years ago I realised that God had called me to minister to women. I was young, my marriage was barely three years old and I was still trying to find my way to a place of fulfillment. I was just beginning to recognise what was important, so to have ministry thrown into the mix was not what I would have chosen. But I heard God clearly say He wanted me to do it!

......I realised that God had called me to minister to women. I was young, my marriage was barely three years old and I was still trying to find my way to a place of fulfillment.

I tried to find someone who understood what I was feeling at the time; inadequacy was killing me! I had no idea who wanted to subject themselves to my ignorance and I definitely didn't want to hear me speak on matters as important as marriage and destiny! But I stepped out all the same. My first set of experiences was not helpful either. I had people who accused me of wanting to start a church to those who clearly told me I was too inexperienced to have anything to offer. My weaknesses were not helping, and I felt surely God couldn't have called me to do this, because it seemed really hard! But every time I had the opportunity to teach, no matter how few the women were, the fulfillment I got made up for all the feelings of rejection and fear.

I knew I needed to find someone who had been there and who could just tell me it was going to be okay. But the sad reality was that I couldn't find anyone who was willing to stop long enough to invest in me and help me find the confidence to continue. I kept telling myself that surely, if I ever did make it in this calling I was going to make myself available to others who will need me.

Then one day I found my kind! Someone brought me a book by Joyce Meyer. I cannot remember the title today, but I do remember that her openness shocked me! I remember saying to myself, this is exactly how I would say it if I was in her position. I thought that if Joyce, despite her struggles could make it this far then surely I stood a chance. She immediately became my sounding board; she became the one with whom I shared my frustrations. No, I didn't have access to her, but her books proved to be very helpful in putting into perspective the issues that I faced, and like Rick Warren, she helped midwife the confidence with which I still stand today. My greatest challenge was recognising how weak and imperfect I was, so having Joyce Meyer talk about her imperfections and struggles so openly made me realise that God will use me if I make myself available to Him. I also realised that He will continue to work on my imperfections along the way, and hopefully one day I will be able to say I have made at least a twenty percent improvement.

The Mary and Elizabeth Collaboration

There is another story like this one in the Bible that will most likely drive this home for you. And it is the story found in the book of Luke 1: 26-56. Mary, the virgin betrothed to Joseph, received a visitation from a divine being. The Bible says an angel appeared to her to tell her that she had been highly favoured by God and so will become pregnant with a child conceived by the Holy Spirit who will be the Saviour of the world! This was great news except for the tiny fact that Mary wasn't married yet, and so stood the risk of being stoned to death should people find out that she was pregnant and Joseph had nothing to do with it! But there was this piece of information, which didn't look relevant, that

But there was this piece of information, which didn't look relevant, that the angel had passed on to Mary as well.

the angel had passed on to Mary as well. Considering the information overload that Mary was receiving at the time, telling her that her cousin Elizabeth was pregnant shouldn't mean so much except when you take into cognizance the fact that Elizabeth's story is peculiar too! I mean everyone had concluded that Elizabeth was barren. I cannot but ask how come it was she who was barren and not her husband Zechariah? Anyway, Elizabeth was pregnant and she was past the age when she should be proudly pregnant! She was over the hill as they say, if you count the fact that the angel said she was pregnant in her old age!

So there they were, two women, one too young and unmarried to justify a pregnancy and the other too old to flaunt a pregnancy! Both of them had joyful news but the circumstances around them would not let them testify to the goodness of God in their lives. In verse 39 of Luke 1, the bible records that Mary got up and headed towards the hill country, to the town of Judah where Elizabeth lived with her husband Zechariah. By the way, if you read Luke 1 from the beginning, you will see how astounding Elizabeth's pregnancy was! It was such a tall order that even though the angel appeared to her husband, the Priest, right at the altar where he was burning incense, he just couldn't understand it. So the angel told him he wouldn't be able to speak until the baby was born! I am thinking that Zechariah was going to be one really negative midwife for his wife Elizabeth. He wasn't going to be able to rejoice in what God wanted to do, neither was he going to be able to positively support her in words, he probably would have blabbed the secret to those who ought not to know, and so God shut him up.

Maybe today, you have great news but sharing it will only ridicule the power of God, as man may not be able to comprehend this move of God, and you are wondering how it will turn out. Elizabeth's story should encourage you. Even when the wrong person lays hold on your delivery status, because he or she is not your midwife, God can and will shut them up! If Zechariah, the father of the child, could not speak until the child was born, just what do you reckon God can do to all those who are around you, and will ultimately share in your testimony but right now are not your midwives? He will shut them up!

Even when the wrong person lays hold on your delivery status, because he or she is not your midwife, God can and will shut them up!

However, Elizabeth still needed someone who could identify with what she faced and so she found Mary or Mary found her. If God will shut somebody out of your birthing process, it is because He has a more qualified midwife around the corner. This is a total and complete walk of faith! So if you will hold on in faith, God Himself will arrange for the ordained midwife to show up. The God we serve is the one who rules in the affairs of men, nothing will slip by Him. He has you covered. The point to note here is that for any two or more people to collaborate to effectively birth destiny together, they have to agree.

Mary and Elizabeth definitely agreed on the fact that the God that they served specialises in impossible feats. For one He caused a pregnancy in what had been categorised a dead womb, and in the other, He brought forth a pregnancy even without sexual intercourse.

The thing is these testimonies can only make sense to those who have experienced something similar and so these women had to connect. I am of the opinion that the angel didn't just tell Mary about Elizabeth's pregnancy to encourage her, but so that she will find succour with her cousin who was going through a similar situation. It goes without saying that because these women went through this path individually, they would know what to say to each other. They would be able to comfort and stand up for each other, rejoice over each other's victories, and cry over their struggles in the months that led to both births. In verse 56, of Luke Chapter one, we are told that Mary, remained with Elizabeth for three solid months. There was a hope in Elizabeth which was not alien to Mary. Your midwife will have a hope within her that connects with the hope within you.

Commonality is the first step towards connecting with the right midwife. Her heart's cry will and must resonate with yours. Midwives are not chosen by the individual in the birthing process, they are pre-ordained by a God who knows the end of a thing from the beginning. Just the same way Joyce Meyer had treaded a path of inadequacy and now stepped out in authenticity; I was looking to walk the same path.

Just as Elizabeth recognised Mary's unique destiny because the baby within her womb bore witness to the baby in Mary's womb, you will recognise your midwife because what you carry in each of your wombs bears witness to what God wants to use you both to achieve for His Kingdom. Hold on.

Something seems missing from this equation. Why didn't Mary discuss the pregnancy with Joseph? Why didn't she ask him what he thought about the matter? She just left the presence of the angel and went straight to Elizabeth. It was simple; only those who have been there can understand what someone else is facing and Elizabeth was the perfect candidate for that. Also, Mary knew it was God alone who would be able to convince Joseph that this was from Him.

......If you will heed the call for collaborations, the first thing you must understand and realise is the fact that this will not happen in a vacuum.

And so Mary left God's work to God and she went to collaborate with Elizabeth for the benefit of the destinies they both carried.

Today, if you will heed the call for collaborations, the first thing you must understand and realise is the fact that this will not happen in a vacuum. It will take groups of people coming together with like passions and similar experiences to birth collective destinies. Like I said about how Joyce Meyer inspired me through her books, it was the similarities that I could point to in our struggles and outlook on life that made her books second only to the Bible at the time. She answered questions about my future like she lived my life before me! Her ability to glean wisdom and learn a lesson from all the things she had to face gave me the confidence to dare to believe that my life will turn out right too. She made me recognise that no one was beyond God's redemption and use and that meant a lot to me.

Back to Mary and Elizabeth, what is it that made their coming together so easy? The moment Mary stepped into Elizabeth's house she (Elizabeth) broke into a prophecy, the baby in her womb leapt for joy and so many other things that were not expressly said in the Bible happened. For me, I will put it like this; they were good for each other! Mary didn't have to try too hard; Elizabeth didn't have to pretend she was super human or spiritual. They both knew what they were faced with, they knew the disadvantages of their peculiar situations but they both had a common focus; carrying destiny to term and bringing forth without a hitch!

There is a commonality in their situation that attracted them to each other like I had pointed out earlier, but what was this common ground about? It was about what God wanted to do. If you noticed, the angel didn't come to ask their permission to bring heaven into earth; he just invaded their lives with it! But they were willing; as uncomfortable and shameful as it was likely to be for both of them, they submitted to the sovereign will of God! Should there have been something that one didn't like about the other, she would have had to put it aside for the sake of destiny.

For you today, as you step out into collaboration, is your partner in anyway like you? I mean do they have the same value system as you? Do they believe in the same God you believe in, are you clear on why they have set out to do what it is they have set out to pursue?

Except you find common ground, I can assure you that once in a while, you may have to face the heat together, are you sure what the other person's response will be? Collaboration, as the Lord has laid it in my heart, is not only about the outcome, it is also about the process. It is a means through which God wants to forge again the unity that has been lost in the body because of cross purposes and selfish interests. The best kind of collaboration is therefore that which will be forged through people who believe in the same thing, and are willing to put their selfish interests aside to push the common goal.

It is about being there for each other and ensuring everyone fulfils destiny. This has become necessary because in the end it is about the big picture which is what God wants to achieve with our individual gifts. No one man can build a house alone! No matter how hard a worker we are, there are aspects of our dreams and destinies that will require other people's input and collaborations to help ensure that destinies are achieved, not only according to God's time table, but also according to His pattern.

For instance, if the Mason says to the carpenter that he is not needed in putting the building up, then how will the roof go up? If the painter refuses the plumber the opportunity to contribute his quota, how will the fittings be put in? We are all called to contribute our quota to making the world a fabulous place for ourselves and others, and the tools to achieve this have been deposited in us as gifts and talents. Collaborations help us identify who we will travel with to birth quality destinies and joining with those who know where we have been or are headed can be a big help.

Mary could have gone home to her immediate family but she didn't, she could have gone to her friends but when it got critical she sought out one who could identify with her, and the struggles she faced.

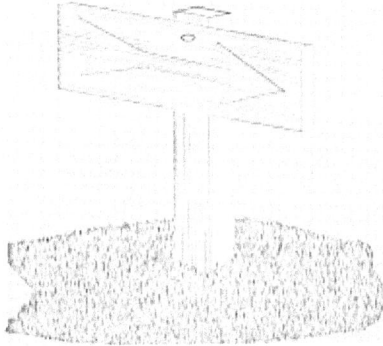

If we will be discerning enough, God will lead us to people who can help us birth our destinies and who will understand the urge we have to make a difference with a God-given and driven destiny.

If we will be discerning enough, God will lead us to people who can help us birth our destinies and who will understand the urge we have to make a difference with a God-given and driven destiny. It is very important that you find someone with common ground in the following areas:

Value System:

This can be defined as a set of cultural and moral values peculiar to a person or group. According to Zorka Hereford, author of EssentialLifeSkills.net, "*a personal value system is a set of principles or ideals that drive and/or guide your behaviour. It gives you structure and purpose by helping you determine what is meaningful and important to you and helps you express who you are and what you stand for. If you are unaware of, or become disconnected from your values, you end up making choices out of impulse or instant gratification rather than on solid reasoning and responsible decision-making."* [1] In a nutshell, your values define your character.

Passion:

The dictionary defines passion as a strong affection or enthusiasm for an object, concept, etc. But Brian Norris (Briannorris.com) delves deeper. He says, *"Passion is a gift of the Spirit combined with the totality of all the experiences we've lived through. It endows each of us with the power to live and communicate with unbridled enthusiasm. Passion is most evident when the mind, body and spirit work together to create, develop and articulate or make manifest our feelings, ideas and most sacred values. It enables us to overcome obstacles (both real and imagined) and to see the world as a place of infinite potential."* [2]

Belief:

This word is defined as having confidence in the truth or existence of something not immediately susceptible to rigorous proof. According to Jerry

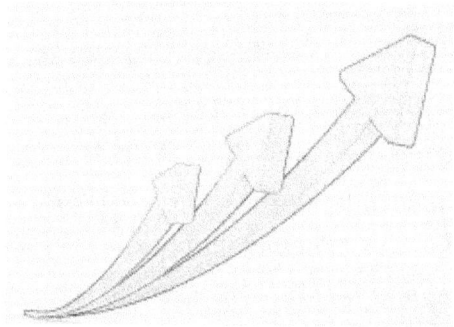

Values, Passion, Belief.....if we are to live by these three guidelines, there is no telling how far we will go and how much we can achieve when we come together......

74

Lopper (101suite.com), *"a belief is a thought we hold and deeply trust about something. They tend to be buried deep within the subconscious with the result that they trigger automatic reactions and behaviours. We seldom question beliefs; we hold them to be truths."* [3]

If we are to live by these three guidelines, there is no telling how far we will go and how much we can achieve when we come together in collaboration to achieve God's desire for mankind. Ruth must have had a personal value system that defined her character (loyalty). She had the passion that enabled her overcome the obstacle of widowhood. She believed in the God Naomi served and believed in Naomi too. She proved this every time she obeyed every single instruction Naomi gave her. By collaborating with the right person, till today, Ruth's name has never failed to be mentioned in the genealogy of Jesus Christ.

Understanding the big picture

Before we delve into what understanding the big picture is, we will try to define understanding and also what we mean by the big picture.

According to an article by Professor Y.K Ip on Successful

Learning, "many people tend to equate 'knowing' with 'understanding' meanwhile they are two different things. He says that *"To understand is 'to comprehend', and to comprehend is 'to take in' or embrace... understanding is a generalized meaning or insight."*[4]

On the other hand, 'Big picture' as defined by the dictionary is an overall view or perspective of a situation or matter.

Having a clear definition on what these two words are, we will be right to say that understanding of the big picture is us coming together to collaborate after we have fully taken in or embraced the overall perspective of our purpose. We need to realise that the purpose for collaboration goes beyond the now; it is pertinent that we have an insight of what God wants to achieve and know that the goal is for the greater good of mankind, even for future generations. When Christ came to earth, He had an understanding of the big picture; His purpose was beyond just saving the lost sheep of Israel, it went as far as redeeming even the gentiles in generations to come. He submitted to God's will and today, He is the only way to salvation and God, the Father. When you submit to God's sovereign will, no matter the hitches you may encounter, your collaboration will turn out well and will yield the desired fruit to the Glory of God.

Action Exercise

i) How would you identify the people who have similar values and passion with you?

ii) If you had a better view of how a Sista can handle her life issues because you have gone through same, how would you help her through it?

iii) What are the most important areas you and your partner in collaboration need to agree on to be able to achieve your goal?

4 RULES OF COLLABORATION

Like everything else in life, collaboration has its rules. And like everything else, most of these rules are unspoken. What I mean is; collaborations are about relationships and few people enter into relationships with a rule book. We all want to get into our relationships believing the best of everyone, and hoping they believe the same about us.

However, when something goes wrong because of something one party did, eye brows are raised and questions are asked. The red flags go up and you suddenly realize that you have fouled a rule during the game. If you are smart and the relationship or collaboration is important to you, you immediately begin to find ways to smooth out the ruffled feathers. If you are not discerning enough, you wonder why people are acting the way they are, because after all there was no rule that said that you should not have acted the way you did. Many great relationship has been messed up

Like everything else in life, collaboration has its rules. And like everything else, most of these rules are unspoken. What I mean is; collaborations are about relationships and few people enter into relationships with a rule book.

because of this. And even though there can never be a rule book comprehensive enough to deal with all the peculiarities that can arise in different collaborations because of the difference in personalities of the individuals involved, it is still extremely important that we all understand what we are doing and why. There is also a need to know what we are willing to do, for the sake of midwifing and co-birthing destiny. Even though I am sure you now know what collaboration is, maybe we should define it one more time. A collaboration is an empowering connection aimed at ensuring that all parties involved win.

Note: each party will bring something different to the table and not everyone will look like they are winning all the time, however, with time the other party's trophy is bound to show up.

The David and Jonathan Collaboration

One story that comes to mind for me is the story of David and Jonathan in the book of I Samuel 18. In this story you'll find that Jonathan was the heir apparent to the throne of Israel. He was meant to take over from his father, Saul, if everything went well. But somehow, Saul missed it and God decided to take the kingdom from him and give it to David.

God wanted better for His people than Saul was willing to do and God required more from His people than Saul was willing to give, but this had nothing to do with Jonathan. The Prophet of the time was instructed by God to go and anoint one of Jesse's sons, who turned out to be David, as King Saul's replacement.

In the course of the story an evil spirit came upon Saul, and David found his way into the palace. Even though Samuel had announced to Saul that the kingdom had been torn out of his hands, he definitely did not tell him to whom it had been given. But Jonathan knew; he just knew that he was out of the game and that David was going to be king in place of his father Saul. Anybody in the flesh would have been upset with both the system and the people involved and definitely would not be willing to partner with the man who was taking away what was his without a fight. But Jonathan approached David and pledged his allegiance. What a strange way to handle the matter. For a man who was not just a soldier but also a crown prince, this definitely was not a manly act. Who gives up a throne without a fight? David was only a shepherd; there was no sense in approaching him to pledge allegiance. In today's logic, what Jonathan should have done would have been to side with his father and give David a run for his money, but

The Prophet of the time was instructed by God to go and anoint one of Jesse's sons, who turned out to be David, as King Saul's replacement.

not Jonathan; he did the exact opposite and was loyal until death!

What did Jonathan ask for in return? Only that David will show him and his descendants mercy when he becomes King! What was Jonathan thinking? Some have argued that he took a defeatist approach because he recognized that he was no match for David and God, but I think that Jonathan was more than the man most of us will ever be!

Jonathan was thinking about what will better serve everybody. He was doing something called Big Picture thinking. He recognised immediately that David's call and assignment required midwives to come into fruition and chose to be a midwife not a 'Pharaoh.' He chose to enable God's will to come to pass and not pursue his own selfish purposes. Jonathan chose that day to collaborate for value not for selfish interest. Today, the mantra is *"what is in it for me?"* And as much as we are talking about winning as individuals, the best kind of winning is when a man or woman puts his or her own selfish desires aside to further the cause of the greater good. There is a definition of the word success I heard and it explains for me what real winning means. "Success when achieved provides opportunity for others." If we are in this to win, we must ensure that our winning adds value rather than hurts others in the process. Jonathan's stance was very important oil in the wheel of the success that trailed David's reign. He saw to it that he alerted David when his father was planning to kill him; he helped him escape and remained loyal to him (compare this to David's own son, Absalom, who rose against his father). He kept his part of the bargain, made himself of no repute just so that God's will for the greater good of all of Israel could come to pass.

Any collaboration, as advocated by this book, should carry in it the seed for the future of not just our children but for the good of generations after us. A wise man once said that even though the things that happen in life appear as dots, in the end the dots connect. I was privileged to have God explain to me a number of years ago, the fact that His purpose for mankind is like a giant art work, and that individual destinies represent a different artist painting his strokes.

In my mind I see that all of life is one very big unfinished picture, and every time I take a step towards making the world a better place, I paint another stroke. It is therefore imperative that each of us paint our own stroke if this picture will be a finished beauty that it was destined to be.

The Jonathan and David collaboration is for me a clear example of how people who are moving with eternity as their goal and focus will act.

Collaborating For Value

It is still extremely important that when you get into collaborations, value is at the back of your mind. VALUE is the Why of Collaboration!

The first reason for getting into any kind of collaboration is to ensure that the purpose for which you are joining forces has the capacity to be a blessing to a part of society no matter how small it is. If you decide to get into a business, then it must be important that you ensure that there is a way your business will impact upon the society. Lately, Corporate Social Responsibility or CSR as it is popularly termed, has become a huge industry because people are beginning to recognise that wherever they conduct their businesses and make profits, there ought to be a conservation of not just the people but even the environment.

The reason why this is suddenly such a big deal is because it was always in the mind of God. When Moses went through the training in Midian as a shepherd, it was for the greater good of the people of Israel. Joseph's experience in the pit, slavery and prison was for the greater good of his family, Israel, Egypt and the world.

Lately, Corporate Social Responsibility or CSR as it is popularly termed, has become a huge industry .....

86

According to John Maxwell 'people really don't care what we know until they know how much we care.' I have found that the more I think about how to add value to those I am dealing with, the better my business gets because somehow, others begin to make it their business to add value to me too.

Not too long ago, I had a wonderful opportunity to join forces with a group of women for destiny and I will never forget that first meeting we had. We were all gathered with our various fears, apprehensions and questions. I was not sure what I was going to get, but I was willing to step out in faith. At that meeting, we all tried to answer the expectation question. For the benefit of others, each of us had to state what we were hoping to gain by this collaboration, and by the time each woman spoke, it dawned on me that we all wanted the same thing.

We all wanted someone to care for and someone to care for us. We wanted someone to rejoice with and who would rejoice with us. We didn't want to fight our battles alone; we wanted to be able to fight as a platoon. We all were looking for people who would laugh with us and not be uncomfortable seeing us cry and maybe even cry with us if need be. We were looking for women who would stand with us irrespective of where the journey of life takes us.

That one exercise opened my eyes to the fact that every

relationship and collaboration has rules and expectations; most of them are just never spoken.

Consequently, when engaging in collaborations such as the one this book is advocating, it is vital that these rules are all spoken and all these expectations voiced. This helps to clarify the vision and hold the individuals involved accountable to their partners and teams.

A few boxes you should be able to check before you collaborate are as follows:

1. What is my purpose? Why am I on earth?
2. What are my strengths? What traits do I possess that are useful in fulfilling my purpose?
3. What things are of value and importance to me?
4. What principles do I hold dear to my heart… what will I accept, what will I disallow?
5. Can I bring myself to be accountable to this individual?
6. What does this person possess that will enhance and add value to my purpose?
7. What will I give back to them? How does my own gift impact on and enhance their dreams and aspirations?
8. How long will I be involved in this collaboration? Am I ready to go the long haul?
9. Am I willing to make sacrifices if need be to give value in this collaboration?
10. What do we want to achieve together?

These may not all be relevant in your peculiar case but I bet more than five of them will be.

When you get into the relationship, there are also a number of things you will want to look out for to ensure that you have a valuable and enhancing collaboration.

Passion

Everything you do must be backed with passion. It is therefore, extremely important that you not only have a passion for what you are collaborating on, but also guard jealously your passion levels. This will ensure that you are not depleted at any point in time no matter the circumstance or challenge you may encounter.

Keep the End in Sight

Once in a while, things will happen within your collaboration that may want to throw you off balance; a great attitude is extremely important. The attitude I tend to adopt is to look at the goal vis-à-vis the issue at hand. With the goal in sight take another step towards achieving what I need intended when I set out. This has helped me work on my relationships and kept me grounded when others were giving up. Remember Joseph's positive attitude to life despite the various challenges he faced with his brothers and in Potiphar's house. This led him to the place of fulfillment God planned for him.

Be Open to Learning

I found out early that the man who refuses to learn new things is the man who is ready to die. So I get into my relationships with the mindset that there must be something I am able to learn from the individual I am joining forces with. Now it is also my mindset that I spend fewer hours in an environment where I am not learning anything. Because of this, I have learnt wonderful things from all kinds of people. From domestic helps, friends and even from school mates. It is important that they have something I can learn. What this means is I am willing to submit myself and it doesn't matter from whom I have to learn. I always say that in the end, the credit always stays with me, so it takes nothing away from me to remain teachable.

In the book of 2Kings 5, Naaman was the Syrian army commander but he was a leper. When asked by the prophet of God to wash in the river Jordan for healing, he got angry. But thank God he had a little bit of humility left in him. He listened to his servant's advice to do as the prophet said and he got what he needed; healing.

God can teach you using any vessel. They could be lower than you in social status or even higher...the point is you must be willing to learn.

God can teach you using any vessel. They could be lower than you in social status or even higher…the point is you must be willing to learn.

Make Growth a Conscious Effort

Sometimes we come out of a formal learning environment and refuse to add any other value to what we already know. To be effective in our collaborations, we have to be hungry for growth; spiritually and intellectually. Daniel said in Daniel 9:1 "I, Daniel, understood by the books…" He studied the books to know what God had planned out for the children of Israel. If he never improved himself through studies, Daniel would not have known what to pray for specifically. Apostle Paul also admonishes us to study always for both our spiritual and intellectual growth (1Timothy 4:13 & 2Timothy 2:15). Every new thing or principle we learn is value added to what we do. Reading must be done regularly, and growth continually measured.

The Ruth and Naomi Collaboration

As great as the David and Jonathan relationship was, there is another that stands out in the bible; the story of Ruth and Naomi. This is a story with very strong emotional implications. A story that borders around love, loyalty and trust between two women from different religious and cultural backgrounds sharing the same tragedy and joy in the end. You need to read the book of Ruth to be able to follow and understand how collaboration works. After Naomi's husband, Elimelech, died, Mahlon and Chilion, both Naomi's sons, married girls from Moab named Ruth and Orpah. Ten years later these young grooms died too. What could Naomi do? She had nothing and no one else to call her own since both her sons died childless. All she could do was pack up what was left and head back to Israel.

Before disaster struck, Ruth and Orpah were the foreigners in the Elimelech family but as things turned out, Naomi became the outsider in Moab. Life just had to go on, so Naomi made the decision to return to her people and urged her daughters-in-law to do the same. But Ruth decided to go with her. She made that heartfelt declaration in Ruth 1:16-17, and when Naomi saw her determination, she decided to let her come with her. Believe it or not, it couldn't have been easy for Ruth to leave her kin and kindred and go with an embittered mother-in-law to a land and people who did not believe in relating with foreigners. Ruth had her work cut out for her. So why did she do it? I believe she must have considered a number of things before reaching this decision but I usually will stick with the fact that she had a goal, clearly defined as found in Ruth 1:16-17. And the bit about wanting Naomi's God to be her God must have been the most important aspect of that goal. It must have been such that in the few years Ruth lived with

Naomi and her family, she had come to know the God of Israel and appreciate the quality of life He was able to give her. Or maybe the Elimelechs represented their God well, and Ruth said to herself 'this is a God worth knowing personally.'

On another thought, she probably had already developed a relationship with God and didn't see how she could sustain that relationship outside of the Elimelech family considering the fact that she came

Life just had to go on, so Naomi made the decision to return to her people and urged her daughters-in-law to do the same. But Ruth decided to go

from a family of idol worshippers. Whatever her reason, it is clear that God had a plan and Ruth, without knowing it, was following the plot as God had written it.

I would like to point out a few things in this story:

1. Ruth had a goal, and it was to ultimately call the God of Israel her God.
2. Ruth had youth and strength where Naomi was old and bitter. So when they got back to Israel, Ruth volunteered to go work in the fields so they could sustain themselves. She must have known that acceptance amongst the people may be difficult to get but she was willing to work hard to provide for her mother-in-law.

3. She conducted herself so well when she went to the field, that it was easy for the workmen to testify to Boaz about her.

4. When Boaz started to favour her, she told Naomi who immediately suggested ideas for Ruth to act on so Boaz could redeem her. Ruth obeyed Naomi to the letter which was an indication that she trusted her and it turned out well for all involved.

These were two women who found themselves in a very bad situation at the beginning of a new mother/daughter-in-law relationship. Rather than allow that to determine how their lives were going to end up, Ruth rose to the occasion by sustaining and building the relationship; and that one decision altered their story forever. Naomi, who had no hope anymore, had her hope and more restored to her. And Ruth, because of her willingness to submit, learn a new way of life and serve the one true God, received a brand new lease of destiny.

What did this collaboration achieve, you may ask. For one it provided the opportunity for restoration to the Elimelech family, and it opened the door for the gentiles to begin to come into the chosen race even before the coming of Jesus. The inclusion of Ruth in the genealogy of Jesus Christ as recorded in Matthew 1:5 is evidence that this collaboration was more than just two women hanging out together because they suffered a common tragedy. Yes, the deaths were the take off point, but it definitely was God working something out in the background of their lives without their knowledge. Even today, as simple and ordinary as our collaborations may look, if we remember that the steps of the righteous are ordered by God, and nothing happens to us that He is unaware of, then it is safe to say that He is able to use our partnerships and collaborations to impact all of mankind and generations long after us.

The inclusion of Ruth in the genealogy of Jesus Christ is evidence that this collaboration was more than just two women hanging out together because they suffered a common tragedy.

This is why I personally believe that when God makes a call such as this one, it is because there is a blessing hidden within it. He wants to use it to bless the individuals who will yield for the greater good of the community or society. Collaborations help us form effective teams for the benefit of the whole. What one man isn't able to achieve alone, he can achieve even more when he joins forces with the right people; especially when it is for the common and greater good

The essence of these collaborations are therefore so that God's will can be made manifest expressly when we join hands and ask God to use us together to make a difference. Never forget, value is the reason why God wants us to collaborate. It also mirrors the Godhead and how the Trinity works together to push the will of the Father. The question, therefore, is this: who will you join with to push God's agenda? Take a look at the story in Genesis about the tower of Babel, and the children of Israel, God said to the host of heaven, *"these people are of one mind and one language and nothing will be impossible for them to achieve once they make up their minds to do it."*[1]

The greatest tool to a successful collaboration will therefore be agreement. Whatever the idea we are trying to forge so long as we are in agreement, with faith in our hearts, no matter the obstacle we will achieve it. There is strength and power in agreeing to come together to make a difference. Collaboration is therefore a coming together of two or more people to further the purpose of God for their lives. The agreement is therefore between you, your collaborator and God who honours covenants and agreements.

Come As You Are

Look around you today, and you will see a lot of counterfeiting. The cars look bigger in the ads; they seem to drive faster than they have the capacity for. Our print media is replete with air brushed and beautifully photo-shopped pictures. The sixty, going on seventy woman has no wrinkles at all. We dye our hair and grey has become an abomination.

Underneath our garments we either tuck the tummies if we have the guts, or we go for 'body magic.' We have been around for so long, but why must we continue to look like we just got here? The days when grey and wrinkles used to mean experience and respect are long gone. We go around thinking we should look young forever even if we don't live forever. Businesses are doctoring their books to look better than they really are. People are borrowing to continue to live the life they only wish they had. There's so much falsehood that we have no idea what to believe anymore. The corporations want to hire those in their twenties with job experiences of a minimum of five years in an environment where it takes a minimum of between six and eight years to acquire a degree in a school where you are not allowed to get in by law before you are eighteen.

We have been around for so long, but why must we continue to look like we just got here?

It is the new life; the one that even children of God have come to adopt. The bigger your church building the better, it seems, your church is. Nobody cares about the message and the Spirit anymore. Those shopping for churches now ask if the church is air-conditioned rather than ask if the doctrines and teachings are based on the Bible.

It is therefore no wonder that even our relationships are fake. People come under so many layers of façade that we cannot exactly say who they are anymore. She comes to visit me in a borrowed car, wearing a borrowed dress, with a berry without black, wearing gold plated jewellery with no gold in them, speaking in a diction I know for sure she doesn't possess, to tell me about her million dollar business she doesn't own and invite me to her mansion she has not paid for... need I go on?

Let's not even talk about the false hair, false lashes... This is the extent of our faking. The question now is; who really am I if I am taken over with so much falsehood? Any collaboration that must work will need to be between real people; flesh and blood people with human challenges and problems. Your partner or collaborator doesn't want to join forces with a perfect person, just a real one.

It is therefore extremely important that the people we are dealing with can attest to the fact that they are dealing with the real us. What this means is that you can relate with them based on the facts about who you are and your authentic personality than to have to keep up with some disguise or the other.

An ability to be real will also empower the other party to deal with you from their position of strength taking into account your own strength as well. Imagine that you got in a collaboration with someone who isn't who they claim to be, it will automatically mean that you cannot trust them to be able to handle the responsibilities assigned to them as they may not even possess these abilities in the first place.

The impact of this on the desired value cannot be over emphasized, because without meaning to hurt the process, pretension and a lack of truth will do just that. This may negate the outcome, and can even cripple the relationship in itself.

Imagine that Ruth didn't know the first thing about harvesting wheat, but she had presented herself to Naomi like she did. And let us say, for discussion purposes, that their life depended on that ability she claimed to possess; how would things have panned out for them?

If Jonathan was not a loyal friend to David as he claimed; if he was actually scheming with his father, King Saul, to set a trap for David so he could be killed, how would David have felt if he found out? If Joseph pretended to be a good boy before Potiphar and the rest of his household but when no one was watching, complied with his master's wife's seductions, he would have ended his destiny as an ordinary slave; if not executed for such a treacherous deed.

Pretence will only weaken your ability to do your best in any collaboration. As you struggle to keep up appearances, you will continue to sink in your own quicksand of self destruction.

Nobody would be able to save you except you accept that you have been living a lie all along and are ready to place your cards on the table. You need to be open and honest with yourself, open and sincere to God your maker (after all He knew you before you were even formed) and sincere with your collaborator. Being an open book is the only way you will be able to attract the right persons into your life to join forces with you in achieving God's purpose for your life and mankind as a whole. Come as you are and see what God will do through you.

Action Exercise

i)   What are the things you've identified that could create friction between you and your partners in collaboration?

ii)   What measures are you willing to take or have taken to quickly resolve these issues?

iii) Between David and Jonathan, who would you identify yourself with in your current relationship with others?

Iv) What is the one thing that can ruin or weaken your ability to do the best in any collaboration?

5 THE ESSENTIALS OF COLLABORATION

Like everything that thrives in humankind, relationships are the foundation of a great collaboration. No matter how shallow a relationship may seem at the beginning, once you have put your foot in the door that relationship has the potential to become a collaboration that can bring about major change both in what you are doing as an individual and to your destiny. Relationships therefore form a major part of the success or otherwise of any collaboration.

The Ruth and Naomi Model

No matter how shallow a relationship may seem at the beginning, once you have put your foot in the door that relationship has the potential to become a collaboration that can bring about major change both in what you are doing as an individual and to your destiny.

Our model relationship that we will be examining to buttress the principles of this chapter, will be the Naomi/Ruth relationship in the book of Ruth. Now, for Naomi and Ruth, theirs was one that evolved into a collaboration to birth destiny. How? They both had the opportunity of being thrust into a relationship by marriage. Remember,

Ruth Married Naomi's son Mahlon, who died a few years into the marriage. It was in the place of this relationship that the connection that brought forth that powerful collaboration was forged.

Now, this may not be as strategic a relationship as we are advocating via this book, but it is apparent that people will only go the long haul with you, based on the relationship you have with them. Ruth must have decided to go back to Israel with Naomi because of what she saw in the few years she was married to her son.

The issue with relationships is that they take a while, sometimes, to forge. They also need work and nurture but in the end, if these are properly deployed, the work will be worth it. Naomi must have liked Ruth, but most likely Ruth loved Naomi. As you will agree with me, love is not something that people give to others at the level at which Ruth gave it without thinking it through. In essence, even what Ruth did with Naomi was strategic.

Bob Burg, the author of the book on networking, The Go Giver has this to say about how winning relationships are forged. "All things being equal, people will do business with and refer business to those people they know, like and trust." This for me is forging a relationship at the beginning to bring about value to both what you are doing and what God has called you to do. Like I mentioned in an earlier chapter, these people become what I call the midwives of our destinies. For people to bring their presence, skill and resource to push what you are doing as an individual, the following elements as outlined by Bob Burg will have to be in place. Who is going to come to your aid or join forces with you except they know you? I have been told a lot of times recently, that the value of what I do, can so easily expand if I open myself to more relationships.

"Everyone knows 250 people, on average, some more and some less. When you do business with just one person and you don't treat them right they will tell all 250 people about the experience.

After people get to know you, can you say they like you and what you stand for? Do they see anything authentic in you and about you that can make them want to join forces with you? When I have the opportunity to teach on Personal Branding, I quickly tell my trainees that what others say about them matters more than they can ever know. This is because of the Law of 250 as propagated by Joe Girard who has been listed on the Guinness Book of World Records as *"The World's Greatest Salesman."* The law of 250 is simple but very profound, because it states that:

"Everyone knows 250 people, on average, some more and some

107

less. When you do business with just one person and you don't treat them right they will tell all 250 people about the experience. If you alienate just one person a day and they tell 250 people..?"[1]

The flip side is also true. If you treat one person right or if one person likes you enough, the 250 people in his circle become, potentially, people who can become part of your circle and whom you can forge valuable connections with.

How does the law of 250 relate with the 'Know, Like and Trust principle' by Bob Burg? Well in my opinion if one person knows you enough to like you, automatically they can bring some value into what you are doing even without directly doing so. All that is required is that they like you enough to tell some of the people in their circle of influence and a new level of collaboration is forged. Let us take a look at two illustrations; the first from the bible.

The Joseph Principle

Genesis chapter 40 records that after Joseph was sold as a slave to Potiphar, Potiphar's wife tried to seduce him because he was a very handsome lad. But because he had the fear of God instilled in him from childhood, he refused to sin against God and his master. But his master's wife unfortunately held onto something that belonged to him and used it as incriminating evidence which landed him in prison. Now while in prison, Joseph was put in charge of everything and everyone in jail because of his good behaviour. However, two top officials of the king's palace (the Chief Butler and the Chief Baker) were imprisoned for offending the king; and through God's divine orchestration ended up in the same cell Joseph was.

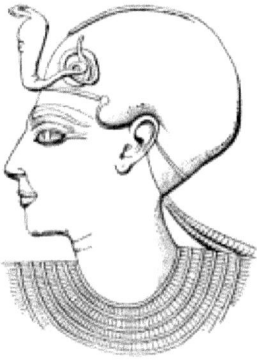

These two people had dreams which Joseph interpreted; the butler would get his job back but the baker would not just lose his job but also his head. Upon his release, Joseph implored the butler to remember him and possibly recommend him to the king and just like the typical human nature, the butler forgot about him until something happened. God caused the king to have a dream that not even the land's greatest magicians could interpret.

God caused the king to have a dream that not even the land's greatest magicians could interpret. God used this to open the door of release for Joseph.

God used this to open the door of release for Joseph. The butler remembered Joseph and recommended him to the king. This recommendation led to collaboration between Joseph and the king to save Egypt and the rest of the world from famine.

A Personal Encounter

The second illustration is drawn from a personal story. A few years ago, I was co-coordinating a weekly program for women in a part of Lagos, Nigeria where I live. And each day after these meetings, I would take a short drive to a weekly market, not far from where the meeting is held, to buy fresh farm produce for my home. Parking was provided for at one spot under the shade of some trees and every week I tend to park at the same spot.

At this spot were usually some young and middle aged men, whom I didn't know but whom I will always politely greet before I go to transact my business. Every day as I return to the car, I will wish them a good day and drive off.

To be honest there was not one of them I might have been able to recognise had I run into him someplace else. I really didn't take the time to relate with them, but I was always polite. This fateful day after the meeting I drove to this market again to buy my farm produce for the week. As I alighted from my car, I noticed that there were more men than usual at the spot, so I did the same thing I usually do every week; politely said 'good afternoon' to them and I went into the market. When I finished shopping and came back to my car, one of the men walked up to me, and I noticed he was better dressed than the rest of them.

After we exchanged pleasantries, he said *"I just want to tell you that you should continue to behave the exact way you have always done."*

At this point, I drew a blank because I had never seen him before, so I wondered how he could have known what it was that I did. Apparently, he noticed that I had no clue what he was talking about so he went on to introduce himself as the Local Government representative for tariff collection at that market and explained that the men I saw every week work for him. He went on to relay to me that his men had told him that every week when I came to the market I was nice and respectful to them. So he wanted to commend me and encourage me to keep being nice.

Yes, I know your next question is what value did this add to me? Well he went on to tell me that should I ever encounter any problem with tariff collectors in that area, I should let him know and he will sort it out. The point is that somehow I have been able to rake up credit in this relationship bank such that whenever I need to use it, I can cash in on it. They knew me a little and obviously liked what they knew about me. Remember that the person I had this conversation with is not any of the people I have related with, even though from a distance. Just like Joseph, I have received a referral from one person low on the rungs of the ladder who has gone on to give the referral to someone a little more higher on the ladder who can affect decision making.

The third step in the 'Know, Like and Trust principle' is the trust level. Once people begin to relate with you at this level, something has definitely hit home and your relationship has indeed become one you are able to cash in on.

More on Ruth and Naomi

Let's return to the Ruth and Naomi equation for a moment. Looking at this relationship, if we consider the background of these two women, they really should not have so much in common. The only thing that bound them was that they had shared mutual love relationships and they had gone through the path of grief together. But there was definitely some mark that Naomi had made on Ruth for her to decide to go along with Naomi even back to the land of Israel where their tradition and culture obviously wasn't welcoming. What I can tell happened here is that Ruth came to trust Naomi enough to put her life in her hands. In Ruth 1:16-17, we see how much Ruth trusted Naomi as exhibited by her proclamation below:

> *"But Ruth answered, "Don't ask me to leave you! Let me go with you. Wherever you go, I will go; wherever you live, I will live. Your people will be my people, and your God will be my God. Wherever you die, I will die, and that is where I will be buried. May the Lord's worst punishment come upon me if I let anything but death separate me from you!" - (GNB).*

Ruth came to trust Naomi enough to put her life in her hands.

I cannot therefore overemphasize the fact that collaborations will be born out of relationships. Since this is so, there is a need to find out how to get into and forge the kind of relationships we are talking about here. Remember these are destiny birthing relationships. What we are talking about here has to do with how far we will push our destinies with the help and assistance of our midwives.

These are therefore strategic relationships; well thought out, nurtured and invested in, and it all begins from the place of a knowing. Do people know what your Vision is; can you articulate it and pass it across? What is the likeability level of your Vision and even of your person? Are you authentic enough for people to trust and want to do business with? Or collaborate with? What Value are you adding even to the individuals you are seeking to collaborate with? And do they know what it is that you bring?

Joseph was authentic enough for the butler to recommend him to Pharaoh; he was trustworthy enough for Pharaoh to do business with and even collaborate with in ruling Egypt.

In his book, 21 Irrefutable Laws of Leadership under the Law of the Inner Circle, my coach and mentor, leadership guru,

John C. Maxwell, says, you ought to pick your inner circle or team (which can also mean your midwives for destiny) with three core traits in mind:

- *Competence*
- *Character*
- *Chemistry*[2]

Let us take these traits one by one and see how they affect the core and quality of our collaborations.

Competence

Here I want us to look at the story behind the lives of the people who you choose to collaborate with. What skills do they possess that are valuable for what you have set out to achieve? What experiences have they had that can enrich what you are working on?

To question the competence of another however, it is taken for granted that you have prepared adequately and have a story, skill and experience that your would-be collaborator might need. Picking your midwives by their competencies enable you make strategic demands on their skills, experiences and stories.

Even if the relationship was forged without our say so, there is still the need for us to look at what we require vis-à-vis what the others bring to the table. God is a God who plans and encourages us to plan. In Luke 14:28-35, Jesus gave the parable of the man who was building but didn't count the cost before he began and because he was unable to finish the building, people began to mock him. This parable is explicit in the fact that the children of God must strategically plan their lives so that efficiency and effectiveness will be rolled into one in the pursuit of their destinies.

Even if the relationship was forged without our say so, there is still the need for us to look at what we require vis-à-vis what the others bring to the table.

However, if I fail to relate competence to the law of 250, then I may not have done justice to the subject matter. Sometimes, the people we will first come in contact with may not have the skill level, experience or story that we desire, but if we still are able to get them to know us, like us and trust us, they may be the key into the referral that will yield the results that we seek. Even though the butler didn't seem to be the right person to get Joseph out of jail, Joseph still got the butler to know, like and trust him and this yielded fruitful results in the end. The golden rule therefore is, as much as it is within our power let us not have people walk away from us with the wrong impression the first time. This is not a call to scurry without dignity but to be authentic.

Character

To understand this trait in getting into the place of collaboration, we need to first define what character is: *"'Character is who we really are. It's what we do when no one is looking. It's the accumulation of thoughts, values, words and actions. These become the habits that comprise our character. That character determines our destiny."*[3]

Now so many different words and traits form the character of a man starting from integrity to honesty, to trustworthiness, responsibility, discipline and a whole lot more. While no part of character is more important than the other, sometimes their ranking on the priority scale should determine what we are looking for in a midwife.

When I met my husband years ago, he had something I had not seen in relationships in a long time, and that was the ability to keep his word no matter what. What this meant was that as long as he gave his word that he was going to do something or be somewhere for you, you could count on the fact that he had said it and will go the extra mile to keep his word.

When I met my husband years ago, he had something I had not seen in relationships in a long time, and that was the ability to keep his word no matter what happened after he had

116

However, there was something else that he kind of struggled with which mattered to me too, and that was keeping to time for appointments. I, on the other hand, was always early for whatever appointment we had. I had to ask myself which was more important on the priority scale for me, and I realised that his ability to come through for me whenever he gave his word was more important.   And today fifteen years later he is on time, and still keeps his word to me.   The point is that depending on what is required from your midwife, you may have to prioritize and stick with the important things.

As much as we want others to be perfect for us, we all are works in progress and if we give people the chance, they may just surprise us over time. In the case of Ruth and Naomi, the Bible records that at some point Naomi became so bitter that she asked people to call her Mara. Who do you think bore the brunt of her bitterness more? The answer is simple. Ruth was the one who had to soak in her bitterness more than anyone else, considering the fact that she was the only person at the time who was close to Naomi. Somehow, Ruth endured or even managed that season of Naomi's life so well. I imagine it must be because somehow she recognised that despite the harsh and bitter front Naomi had adopted because of what life had dealt her, she was a sweet woman inside and had what it takes to come through when it mattered. The point of this is that, as much as we want midwives with character, some midwives will still have flaws because they are human. The butler, who was one of Joseph's midwives, totally forgot about him. This was not deliberate but a clear example of human flaw. When a critical situation came up, however, he quickly remembered he had given Joseph his word. We can look at the case of Miriam too. Consider Miriam, the girl who by the river bank watching her brother to ensure that he was safe and Miriam, the woman who championed a rebellion against the same brother, which earned her leprosy, you will understand that perfection isn't the name of the game. Destiny and grace however, are the main factors here.

Chemistry

This refers to the synergy with which you can relate with your would-be midwife. Your midwife will not be a clone of who you are, or your exact type of person but you must agree on the fundamentally important issues. For instance your beliefs must dovetail. The Bible in Amos 3:3 asks a very fundamental question; *"Can two work together except they be in agreement?"* If your beliefs don't see eye to eye with your midwife's, the tendency then is that your values will defer. I have also found that to determine a synergy of values, the individuals may have to have had time together, to ask questions and proactively determine if they can work together. If for instance family is important to you as an individual, then you must be sure that your midwife or collaborator understands what you mean by saying that family is both important and valuable to you. To help them further understand what you mean, you may have to pinpoint ways in which you will prefer for your family to be treated and dealt with.

This helps to clear the air and keep the important stuff important, and ensures that there is no ambiguity in your use of terms and terminologies. This also helps to set the tone for how your relationship will be nurtured and built.

Recently, I was trying to explain this to my teenage son, and he said to me that making and picking our friends should not be that scientific. My response to him was that we get in trouble with our relationships because over time we have picked our companions without a thought. Taking time to determine what the relationship can achieve based on these three words above will definitely give the relationship a head start.

Measuring a Healthy and Beneficial Relationship

I choose to call these the Es of a relationship. These are words all beginning with E, and can be used to determine if a relationship is good enough to progress into collaboration.

Evaluation

We are working on how to strategically position ourselves so that we can find help and support for God's dreams in our hearts. However, before we begin to take our relationships into the 'collaborating for destiny' mode, we have to evaluate. This means we need to appraise what we are doing and how the individual in question may be a support. This can be likened to due diligence or feasibility study when starting a business. Evaluation is important so we will be able to deploy our relational resource in the right direction.

Empowerment

Like the Ruth and Naomi connection, relationships can be foisted on the individuals involved. Naomi may have had her son Mahlon, but she definitely didn't pick his wife, Ruth. She could have decided that the only thing that would bring them together would be the person they mutually loved, and the moment he died that would have been the end of the relationship. After all, Orpah chose not to go with Naomi. The question then becomes why did Ruth stay?

Empowerment in any relationship is very key; if you allow these kinds of people into your destiny to act as midwives, they will do well by you.

I believe that as human beings we tend to gravitate towards people who empower us, either with their words or the things they allow us do around them. I have benefited immensely from such a relationship with my husband, Mark. He has always supported me even when I couldn't support me! He is quick to tell me he believes in what I can achieve and he makes commensurate sacrifices to prove that he means what he says. He is therefore my go-to person. I can be sure that no matter what happens, he is going to support me in birthing whatever aspect of my destiny needs to be birthed. Ruth stood by Naomi, possibly because Naomi had been a really great mother-in-law, and that empowerment made it easy for her to make her own sacrifices when she needed to. In the end she got written into the wonderful plan of God. Empowerment in any relationship is very key. If you allow these kinds of people into your destiny to act as midwives, they will do well by you.

Enjoyment

Here is another word that I absolutely love. A lot of our friends say that Mark and I are not fun-loving people because we don't go out much. This is probably because we enjoy our own relationship so much we tend to think we don't need others. We love to read, and discuss the books we read. We are never tired of spending time before God, and we, most importantly, have the same heartbeat when it comes to what God wants us to do; this makes for a great relationship. We make time to enjoy the things that are mutually important to us. For a while, a lot of people thought I just bragged about my husband, but by the time you spend time with me, and he is constantly calling to find out what I am doing, you know we have a mutually enjoyable relationship. It is no wonder he is a great midwife for my destiny.

Recently, God released into my life a new support system comprising five amazing women. Each of them hold a different candle to my heart and each of them are sounding boards and support for different angles of my destiny. We are all serious minded people running our respective businesses and pursuing our individual dreams, but whenever we find the time to come together, it is a feast of enjoyment. And that qualifies them as midwives for my destiny and I hope it qualifies me as a midwife for their destinies as well.

Enabling

Growing up I had some people - thankfully not those whose opinions mattered a lot - who never saw anything good in me. I agree I was not the best behaved teenager on the block, but I also don't think I deserved what they said to me and about me. However, I also had a few relationships that were enabling at that time. I had an uncle who kept telling me that as long as I keep dreaming, I will achieve. I had parents who, even though were not perfect, knew how to validate and stand by me when the going got tough for me. All of these relationships forged an enabling environment where the seed of who I have become today was sown and tended.

When my son was in the lower primary classes, he was very slow in writing and didn't seem to be able to put his sums together. He also had a Mathematics teacher who, when he was in primary four, kept telling my son that he didn't have it in him to do well in Mathematics. One day I walked in on my son weeping profusely in class, and when I asked him what was wrong his exact words were *"Mommy, I don't know what is wrong with me, everybody seems to get it and I alone cannot get it."* It broke my heart. By the time I sought the teacher and found him, he repeated the exact words my son had just spoken. I turned around, went to his class and asked my son to pack up everything that was his, and we went home.

The next week we found another school. Even though my son didn't do too well in the entrance examination his new class teacher, Mrs. Ebea, assured me that she would attend to him personally. She gave him personal lessons and kept telling us that my son was one of the brightest children. By the end of the session till recently, when my son finished Junior Secondary School, he has never again struggled with his mathematics.

Reason? One woman gave her word and created for him an enabling environment where he could soar and manifest the fulfillment of his destiny. That was a midwife, and my family is eternally grateful to her.

Encouragement

What Mrs. Ebea had, and the teacher in the previous school my son attended didn't have, was the ability to keep encouraging the lad rather than talk down at him and tell him he didn't have it in him. The bane of most relationships is a lack of encouragement and I can assure you that it is 'destiny suicide' to align your dreams with someone who never sees something to encourage you for. Every great relationship that will do well as a collaboration will definitely be one where the parties involved understand the need for mutual encouragement.

One woman gave her word and created for him an enabling environment where he could soar and manifest the fulfillment of his destiny.

There is no dream, no matter how small, that is a walkover and Bruce Wilkinson in his book, The Dream Giver, tells how there are forces assigned to every dreamer to discourage him so he will give up on his pursuit. My mindset is this: I already have those spiritual forces fighting me, so if I will be in a relationship with anyone, encouragement is something I will be requiring of them.

Please note that these Es are not exhaustive, you can add your own and find out for yourself if the people in your life qualify as midwives for your destiny.

At the same time, if any relationship you plan on starting does not embody the five Es mentioned, then such relationships need to be checked and possibly avoided. If it's already started, it can be disconnected. When an electronic device is plugged into a faulty socket and is not disconnected as soon as possible, it could blow up the device or cause more damage. This can be likened to a relationship that is not beneficial to you. When Naomi decided to return to her home town, Ruth and Orpah were given more than enough reasons to stay back with their people in Moab. Ruth insisted on going with Naomi while Orpah, after a little pressure, disconnected from the trio. There was no regret whatsoever on Ruth or Naomi's part after Orpah left them.

Orpah's disconnection from Ruth and Naomi, I would say, was a blessing to them. Why? You may ask. Have you considered what Ruth's story would have been like if Orpah had joined them back to Bethlehem? Competition for Boaz's attention might have brewed between both ladies. Naomi could have found herself separating fights and mending relationships between them. Whatever you may picture happening between these two ladies, the result would not be what we have today. There would have been no King David and maybe Ruth's name might not have extended to the New Testament where she's mentioned in the genealogy of Christ.

Disconnecting, whether from your end or not should be seen as a blessing and not a curse, especially when nothing beneficial is being gained from either side.

Finally, for this chapter, you will find that I used the word destiny a great number of times and it is deliberate. I feel in my spirit that God wants us to understand that these collaborations and relationships are for one purpose and one alone, so that we can all come into the fulfillment of our individual destinies. That is why the greatest alphabet concerning relationship is the alphabet D. Do the people you are collaborating with recognise that all that you are doing with them is to launch both your destinies? Do they recognise how important destiny is for you? Do they express their willingness to get in the trenches with you to ensure that you have a smooth take off and landing? Destiny is the reason I put my pen to paper. I know this book will help some of you fulfill the yearning in your heart, and I recognise that. Conversely, do you know why you're reading this book? Maybe it will help you identify whose midwife you ought to be. Whatever the case, let us not forget that the entire essence of man and mankind is to give God pleasure and glory. In aligning ourselves with this, I can assure you that you most definitely are fulfilling your destiny.

Action Exercise

i) On a scale of 1 to 10, how would you rate your relationship with people?

ii) After people get to know you can you confidently say they like you and what you stand for?

iii) Have you ever been recommended by someone you related within the past?

iv) Aside from the five Es of relationships listed in this book, can you add at least two others that you can use in measuring a healthy and mutually beneficial relationship?

v) Are you currently in a relationship that is not beneficial to you? If yes, then what steps are you taking to disconnect from it?

6
DESTINY, TALENTS AND STRENGTHS

G oing by the last chapter, it is clear that we can only collaborate successfully if we are real and able to earn the trust of those we are dealing with. This is so important because collaboration is a business of destinies.

We are called into each other's lives to ensure that God's purpose for us and our individual destinies are fulfilled. Why is

it important that we fulfill destiny? Okay, maybe out of a selfish desire to make it, I need to fulfill my destiny, but of what benefit is it to me if the next person fulfils hers? Isn't life about individual journeying? How can the way I conduct my life enhance another person's ability to live and achieve their own destinies?

We are called into each other's lives to ensure that God's purpose for us and our individual destinies are fulfilled.

If you take into account the fact that all destinies are related, then it will begin to make sense to you that what happens to those I relate with can affect my own destiny. Remember how I

131

said that God explained to me that His purpose for life is one big artwork and every one of us has a stroke to paint? Well, if I am selfish enough to concentrate only on how well I can do what I am called to do don't you think that another person's stroke can alter the result that I am meant to get? It is kind of like an assembly line where you have different people working from different points on different machines but all of them are working on one and the same product. Take for instance, at a shoe manufacturing plant, the designer has designed a pair of shoes nine inches high, but can only be bearable to wear by the end user if it has platforms that are at least five inches high in front. Imagine that this has been approved and the person responsible for the top of the shoe has finished his work, and passed it on to the person responsible for the front part of the heel. Imagine that this person decides, for selfish reasons, he is not willing to craft a five inched platform for the front and crafts a three inched platform instead. Now each person has received their piece of specification without the complete shoe design and the last piece of the puzzle lies in the hand of the person who crafts and attaches the actual heel which is meant to be a nine inched heel.

This last assembly worker puts the nine inch heel and the shoe is passed as finished and released into the market. Because I like shoes a lot, I can assure you that a nine inch heeled shoe with a three inch platform will not be comfortable at all and if end users complain, that entire range will have to be recalled! The verdict will be that because one person within the chain did not stick to the specifications, something went wrong that affected the final product.

The above example can be likened to the destiny of an individual and somebody could be responsible for the failure of that person in fulfilling his or her destiny. Every player needs to understand why they are called, and what they are specifically called to achieve. In 1 Corinthians 12:14-26, we find that the reason why the body is made of different parts is so that the wellbeing of the entire body is guaranteed. The legs have their role, just as the hands, eyes, nose, mouth etc. have their roles to play. Imagine that one decides that they are not willing to continue to carry out their function, maybe because they don't feel that their function is important enough or something like that. The Bible is clear that what will ensue will be a disaster of sorts. My point is each one of us here on earth is called to give God pleasure.

We are all called to deliver to God a weight of glory that cannot be questioned by any power; which brings me to the next point. How do we deliver this weight of glory considering that we are all different and have lived different lives and are still walking different paths even today? The diversity and uniqueness with which each one of us has been created, is the reason why the enemy is able to keep us apart. The devil has somehow made us believe that we are so different that we cannot come together to do anything significant. But that is exactly the opposite! Our differences rather than keep us apart are meant to help us see how much we need each other and what great difference we can make if we agree to come together.

It is for this reason that the devil makes us see each other as competition rather than complimentary gifts. Our destinies, though different and peculiar to us, all come together to fulfill God's greatest and most important purpose on earth which is to give Him glory and make the world a better place for us all.

A typical example is still the Ruth and Naomi connection. These women came from very different cultural and religious backgrounds but were able to capitalize on their differences by using it to bring Glory to God. Through them (Ruth in particular), God established the throne of David through which the Saviour of the world was born.

God knows what stroke of the picture He wants each one of us to paint, so He gives the ability to paint that exact stroke.

Or what can you say about Joseph's partnership with Pharaoh in ruling Egypt and saving the world from famine? Even in the world today, we see how the enemy ensures that nations don't agree with nations, tribes disagree with tribes just to ensure that we never speak with one voice. The idea, I believe, is where the devil is concerned. As long as we cannot agree on one course of action, then the weight of glory we are created to deliver will not happen and this makes the devil win.

Talents as Tools for Destiny Fulfillment

Now where is the place of talents, when we talk about fulfilling purpose within our individual destinies and collective walk together?

Destiny is meant to be lived out, and the tools through which we live out destiny are the talents that God Himself deposited within us from the beginning of time. God knows what stroke of the picture He wants each one of us to paint, so He gives the ability to paint that exact stroke. This ability is known as talents. Now some of us rather than explore and exploit this ability or talent to the glory of God, either keep it hidden or disregard it while wishing that they possessed someone else's ability.

What happens therefore is even though God has called us to contribute a particular thing and has equipped us to make that specific contribution, for selfish reasons, we choose different paths and this hurts the overall purpose of God. Collaboration is God's way of helping us see the importance of what we carry, and the significance of our contributions when we join forces with the right people to do what God has ordained for us to do. The Godhead as you know is three in one, also known as the Trinity. To encourage us go far in the place of collaboration, the Trinity has been and will always be a prime example to follow.

Harvey Mackay author of Dig your Well before you are thirsty says "if everyone in your network is the same as you, it isn't a network, it is an anthill." The point he is trying to make is this - for collaborations to work as ordained by God, there is a need to encourage individual strengths and abilities. We all have something to contribute, and the capacity to make our specific and peculiar contributions is hidden within our frame and within our strengths and our talents. What this means is that before we get into collaborations we should be looking for those whose peculiar gifts we require to merge with ours so that we can add value and make a difference in our society.

The Deborah, Barak and Jael Collaboration

There is a story in Judges 4 that brings home to us the principle of operating within our strength zones, and it is the story of Deborah, Barak and Jael. Barak was the commander of the Israelite army at the time and the nation was under Canaanite

SISTAPOWER

oppression. Deborah was the Judge, and things were really bad. The Lord told Deborah that He was going to give the Canaanites into the hands of the Israelites and asked that Barak go out to fight them. Barak however, had fright issues. He had witnessed so much defeat from the Canaanites that he was not willing to venture out except he had God's representative with him on the battle ground. This was understandable but to God, who had spoken a promise, it must have been a lack of faith. God told Deborah to go with Barak but to also let him know that he (Barak) was no longer going to take the victory of Sisera's death but that He (God) was going to deliver Sisera to a woman. And so Jael, a house wife and tent maker comes into the picture. Even though Israel had a female judge, in the person of Deborah, we do not see Jael or any other woman for that matter question why she was the judge and not them. Jael was in her tent minding her business when Sisera, fleeing from the battle ground, showed up at her tent. She knew he was the commander of the enemy army but he was also a friend of her family. Bible says there was peace between Sisera and the house of Heber, the Kenite, who was Jael's husband. She offered him a place to rest, a bowl of milk and covered him with a mantle and he fell asleep.[1]

At this point God's plan kicked into action. Whether Jael knew at the start of that day that the enemy will be delivered into her hand, the Bible does not tell us, but was Jael ready?

With the events that unfolded shortly after Sisera fell asleep, we can say she was prepared and ready.

What I can deduce from this is that sometimes, our collaborations may not look like they are that significant. I mean how does offering the man a place to rest and a bowl of milk qualify as the beginning of the end for the enemy? But Jael was in her place. She could offer that, and she did! For us therefore, even when we may not have the whole 4-1-1 on what is about to happen, sometimes in collaborating, we just have to trust that God knows what He is doing!

Imagine that when Deborah heard God was going to deliver the enemy into the hands of a woman she automatically swung into action, taking up a sword and rushing into the battle front rather than standing on the sidelines praying, like she should do as the judge. I mean if God is giving the enemy into the hands of a woman, what woman better qualifies than Deborah herself; Judge and Prophetess in Israel?

But Deborah understood that if God had spoken then surely He had a vessel prepared. Her responsibility was to go with Barak and stay with him, everything else would be handled by God at the right time, through His prepared vessel. If you were Deborah, how easy would it be to trust that God would pick the right midwife in this case? And if the commander of the army is to be delivered into the hands of a woman, wouldn't a woman in the military be the perfect fit? Jael had an ability no one would have thought to deploy in this situation though. Remember she was a tentmaker? Part of her job was to drive pegs into the ground when tents are being set up. She had done this for so long that it was possible for her to do it in her sleep. She didn't need a manual, she knew exactly where and how to place the peg, she knew how to hit it, and what force to apply to ensure that it goes in at the first drive. And that was the skill she deployed when Sisera came calling. Jael stuck within her strength zone; she didn't look for armour that wasn't fit for her. She knew how to use tent pegs and that was what she limited herself to. Even in our collaborations, we do not need new skills. We may need to learn new stuff, but our collaborations will not be necessarily based on the new stuff we learn, it will be based on what we already know and have done over the years.

Stay In Your Strength Zone

Collaborating from our strength zone is about using skills and abilities that are organic to us. Any collaboration requiring you to reinvent yourself to fit into it is definitely not meant for you. Remember again that God has made you and put within you the talents and abilities that you require to deliver the weight of glory that He desires from you. When He makes a way and puts you within circles where you can contribute, one litmus test is that you will only be required to contribute who you are and what you already know.

Recently, I got into some network and I really wanted everyone to be impressed by what I could contribute. This put undue pressure on me, because I kept trying to reinvent myself to fit the new wheel. One day it dawned on me that if God has placed me here, then He knows they need me just the way I am. Being in that group is ordained of God but changing to become what I perceived is required was a mistake.

God made me understand that if I will remain myself, when my opportunity comes, like Jael, I will have my day. This realisation helped me retrace my steps and I stopped working to be more than I thought I was, and this was a major liberation for me.

In the same vein, when David met with Saul and he offered to go out and confront Goliath on behalf of the children of Israel, Saul figured he had to do something to help David so he offered him his armour. Even though for a soldier this was the ultimate gift, for a simple shepherd boy, it was an impediment. The Bible records that when David wore the armour, it was so big for him that he could not move. David was able to take Goliath down because he was sensible enough to

Being in that group is ordained of God but changing to become what I perceived is required is a mistake.

140

return to the sling and the stones; simple but effective tools that he was both used to using and had won with in the past.

If you made it before your group or within a partnership opportunity, it is time to trust that you have got what it takes and is needed. Within the collaboration is not the time or place for re-inventing yourself or the wheel for that matter. Barak lost out of the honour that God had prepared for him, simply because he didn't trust enough, both in his abilities and in God's word.

If you are the ordained midwife for another's destiny, it is time to believe that God picked you because you have what it takes and because He has prepared you already. Imagine that Jael tried to use a spear or a sword to kill Sisera; maybe, just maybe he would have woken up and killed her before she could put an end to him. Remember he was a seasoned army commander and she was just a tent maker. She had to remain within her strength zone and that was how she won. For you to win for your partner, you must also remain within the confines of your strength zone and your calling.

It is therefore, important to ensure that when someone approaches you to collaborate, what they are asking you to do is hinged on what you have been doing and you have a track record of winning with.

Remember again that it is all about destiny, and to be able to fulfill destiny, we have to look not outside but within us, to discover the grace, gifts and talents that God has placed within us even from before the foundations of the earth.

Action Exercise

i)   Why must we fulfill destiny?

ii)   What benefit is it to you if you helped another person fulfill her destiny?

iii) Should our differences and diversities pose as strengths or weaknesses in our collaborations?

iv) Have you taken out time to identify those with special gifts /talents with whom you can collaborate so as to add value and make a difference in the society?

7
HOW NOT TO COLLABORATE

It was one of the worst times in the history of a nation known to be great and dreaded by its neighbouring nations. Livestock in Israel, both permissible and forbidden, had become extinct. Edible crops had withered; the nation's food basket was nothing but a wilderness. The famine was so bad that the rule of the game became survival of the fittest. Anything anyone could do to survive the extremely tough times was welcome. People had all kind of ideas and they did their best to ensure that they remained alive. It was no longer about amassing wealth and making a name - it was all about staying alive!

People had all kind of ideas and they did their best to ensure that they remained alive. It was no longer about amassing wealth and making a name - it was all about staying alive!

Every human; man or woman, boy or girl, had to fend for themselves. Parents could no longer protect their children and the children couldn't count on their parents anymore, in fact whomever God didn't help was finished. The government of the day was just as helpless as the people they were governing. The king had no idea what to do anymore and to make matters worse, he could not boast of the best relationship with God at that point so, in his mind, it was a no win situation.

Imagine the ingenuity of two ladies who agreed to collaborate. They agreed to make their resources available to each other so as to stretch their life span. And since it was an era of "every man for himself" hence, no eyes watching them, they decided they were going to do it their way.

They thought up a really great idea called sharing. The only thing is they were not sharing their store of wheat nor were they sharing their stash of corn meal; they agreed to share their children. No, not to use them as child labourers in exchange for money, but to kill and eat them! Yes, you got that right, they were going to kill their children one after the other and eat them to stay alive. What!? How monstrous and barbaric can a mother be? Kill and eat her child? I wish I could explain this, but I guess they were in a desperate situation, and their circumstance called for desperate measures. They agreed to kill the first woman's child, cook and eat and when they ran out of that meat, they would do same with other woman's child; hopefully, at the end of that time, the famine would have lifted.

It is not the best plan, I know; in fact it is not a plan any parent should consider but it was the only one these women could come up with. If this is any consolation, at least they agreed to do it together, which means they collaborated.

Well, even that didn't last, because sooner than they expected, the meat from the first child ran out and it was time to kill the next child. But there was a little snag; the mother of this child had a change of heart. She suddenly had a rush of love for her child and could not go through with killing her for meat. At last! Some sanity was setting in and this was a good thing wouldn't you say? But wait; they had an agreement didn't they? Of course they did but unfortunately this other lady backed out of the agreement not minding that she would hurt the other person in the process. [1]

The point of collaborations is to come together and ensure that destinies are birth in everyone concerned. But more importantly, collaborations are meant to bring about an

If I join forces with you, it should be because our combined efforts will enhance and create more value for the common good.

enhancing of the common good. The reason why this is even the subject matter of this book is because as I had stated earlier, God wants to use us to achieve more together. This brings to mind the acronym for the word TEAM; Together Each Achieves More. So with collaborations, we are meant to come together and achieve more.

But even beyond achieving more, we are meant to come together for the common good. If I join forces with you, it should be because our combined efforts will enhance and create more value for the common good. This is why the story of the two women you just read has been set as the template for how not to collaborate.

For starters, what gain is there in parents killing their children for food? None! Nobody but the parents at the time seemed to have something to gain and even that is debatable. Most people will not see any good in this. So without mincing words, you will agree that this collaboration had no value at all, except for the selfishness of two women.

However, let us put aside the morality of this story for a while and analyse this kind of collaboration based on the rules stated in the earlier chapters. If both women had agreed to the terms of their collaboration, how come one of them reneged when it got to her turn to give up her child? Taking it a little further; has this ever happened in your own collaboration? Have you ever given your word and reneged or has someone ever given you their word only to refuse to fulfill it? How did it feel in both situations? The Bible says that even when a man swears an oath to his hurt, he should keep his promise. [2] This is the hallmark of righteous living and anyone who enters into an agreement only to break his or her promise certainly lacks integrity. Beyond all of this however, is the issue of the common good.

Collaborations must always have as their focus, value added beyond any of the individuals needs. The question therefore becomes; how do we collaborate?

The Folly of Conspiracy

It is another day, another era but the circumstances are similar. In 2 Chronicles 20, three nations had come together to fight against the children of Israel and King Jehoshaphat had no idea what to do. The king knew that his army was no match for the three strongest and deadliest armies of the time. So he ran to the greatest ally any man can have. He ran to God and asked for help for his people and God came through for them.

But let us look at what these three nations were trying to achieve. Once two or more people come together and agree to do a particular thing, it becomes a collaboration. When the said project is positive we applaud their collaborative efforts but when it is negative, we call it a conspiracy. So the three nations conspired to put down the children of God. The truth of the matter is that they deployed the exact same principles that a collaborative effort would deploy. They agree to a plan, each nation makes their contribution both in human and financial resources. They agree on who has better skills in different areas of warfare and

The King knew that his army was no match for the three strongest and deadliest armies of the time.

151

make deployments according to their strengths. They even agree on how to share the spoils of war up front.

So in a manner of speaking, they were following the rules of engagement to the letter but rather than use their efforts to add value, they were going to use it to destroy a people that God had a covenant with. In other words, they were working against the plans and purposes of God.

Now when King Jehoshaphat ran to God, God gave him a formula; send your people ahead of the army and let them praise me. Once this happens, I will utterly destroy your enemies. And the Lord God Almighty set an ambush for the five nations and their armies and rather than fight the Israelites they turned on each other and destroyed themselves. What is the lesson for us here? We cannot afford to come together in collaborative efforts against God's plans and purposes. Or should I say conspire? It just doesn't work. Because God says that He watches over His word to perform it! Whatever He has ordained He is able to bring to pass. What we do when we join forces or conspire against God's plan for mankind, is simple... we draw a battle line between us and the most high God. It is usually no secret what the result of such battle will be. When God chose the children of Israel and set them up in the place of a forever covenant, He also expressly warned that once His anointing was upon them no one should even try to touch them... *"Touch not my anointed and do my prophet no harm."*[3]

Now every child of God is a Prophet and an anointed king by God Himself![4] Any attempt for us to join forces in bringing them down is tantamount to inviting the God of the universe into battle and again we all know what the result of such a battle will be.

Even in our present time, the Palestinian nation can tell you how many losses they have suffered in their several wars against the nation of Israel. As small as they may appear on the map, Israel always finds a way to keep their enemies in their place. By now, every right thinking individual needs to understand that it is not about the arsenal or the military force of Israel, but it is about a covenant that some people think is a fable.

Numbers 23:9 is very clear! God is not a man that He should lie neither is He a son of man to repent of His promises. God does not make promises that He cannot fulfill. He never does. As long as He has spoken it, He will ensure that all things work together for the good of His called, towards the fulfillment of His promises in their lives.

Remember Joseph and his brothers? God spoke something into Joseph's life that they didn't even think he deserved or qualified for, so they collaborated (conspired) to ensure that it didn't come to pass. But because this was about Divine destiny, every step they took to foil God's plan for Joseph only helped in bringing him closer to his place of fulfillment.

Growing up, a lot of people told me that I didn't stand a chance. It was not because they hated me, (at least some of them did not) it was because they could not see beyond who I was at the time. They had no idea what God had spoken into my destiny; all they could see was the devil's hold upon my life, so they wrote me off. They told me I was never going to make something out of myself, but that was because they didn't know that it was not my job to make something out of myself! It was God's job and my part was just to agree and align myself with His plans.

It was not because they hated me, it was because they could not see beyond who I was at the time.

Monument vs. Movement

In Genesis 11, the children of God wanted to become a very great nation; they didn't want to lose their essence and their roots. They wanted generations to remember that they lived. So they decided to build a tower that reached to the heavens; a monument that would allow for them to be ingrained and engraved in history forever. Their dream was not altogether a bad one, the reason for this collaboration was laudable, but it was not God's plan. They wanted to build a monument, but God wanted a movement. He wanted them to go out spread to the nations and build men! They wanted to build towers, God wanted to use them to build destinies. They wanted their strength to be concentrated at one spot to become a point of reference but God wanted them scattered all over, so that no nation will be devoid of the manifestation of the sons of God.

So God scattered them and confounded their language! He threw confusion into their midst, He divided them into small groups, no one effective enough to build a tower by themselves, just so that they would step out of their comfort zone and begin to spread to the uttermost parts of the earth.

Today men and women are still building monuments instead of building men! We want people to know what we have achieved by our own making, and we go to great lengths to protect that which we are building. We want to show forth God's glory by the things we do. God on the other hand is calling us, to a deeper level of involvement in His plan for mankind. God wants us to be an extension of His hand beyond the places where we have ability as individuals. He sees that there is great power when we come together, but He wants us to come together for the right reasons.

Take a look at all three biblical examples presented above and one common factor runs through them, the factor of SELF. It is for our own selfish reasons that we do not want to join forces. We believe that having our name on the door is what makes others see the glory that God has put within us. While I do not have anything against our names on the door, it freezes my bones to think of what we do to ensure that the dream happens.

If the Godhead worked as a team and still works as a team today and always will, isn't it obvious that the concept of teams and collaborations is from God?   Our denominations are doing their best to be so different that we forget the people we have been called to care for. The struggle for the glory is so much that we trample on the souls we were called to save. It is rare to see a consortium of denominations working together long enough to achieve any one thing. Once the time for glory comes and all names are not chiseled on the wall, the collaborative effort scatters.

The doctrines of men will not allow the denominations to do their work, because someone finds it difficult to agree with the other on the modus operandi. Should we stand to pray or sit? Should women be allowed or not? Do we pray once a day or ten times a day? Methodology has systematically robbed us of the mandate that God has committed into our hands.

To salvage the situation, God is pushing the original plan; the plan of calling individuals who will agree to team up irrespective of whose name is on the door. God wants men and women who understand that it is not about them, it is about the kingdom of God.   He has quickened our different and individual hearts to ignite and recognise that we are the remnant that the world is waiting upon to manifest. The answer is in us pushing beyond all the things that used to hold us bound and moving into God's agenda for this season.

Redefining the Bottom Line

The reason why a lot of people may not know how to act within collaborations may just be because they have no idea what the bottom line is. Every business has a bottom line and in simple terms the bottom line can be referred to as the most important reward that the business has to offer.

Most people see money and amassing of wealth as the ideal bottom line. Everyone wants to be able to make money, build big houses and buy fast cars, expensive clothes and jewellery. Not that any of it is wrong; but as Midwives of destiny, our bottom line varies from the generally acclaimed ones. Midwives are in the business of aiding to birth destinies which means that our bottom line does not read in dollars and pounds, Euro or Naira; our bottom line is God's purpose for mankind. It was Dr. Myles Munroe who said that the main reason why God put man on earth is to invade earth with the

Most people see money and amassing of wealth as the ideal bottom line.

Kingdom.

What this means is that when we set out to collaborate, we must understand that it is not about us. Yes, it is impossible for us to collaborate for other destinies without benefiting in the process, but the benefit is not the reason we step out. We step out because we have heard God speak to our hearts what we should do and whom we should do it with.

We step out because God has put dreams in our hearts and we recognise that to be able to make the desired impact, we should join forces with other people with the same dream. Aligning our bottom line with God's means that we hold dear and important what God holds dear and important. We begin to see the world the way God sees it; we should be asking what we can do to make it better rather than what we can get out of it.

To understand how to align and redefine our bottom line to suit God's heartbeat, there are a number of issues we can think through. We need to understand why we agree to do what it is that we want to do. We should think through on who benefits and what they benefit. This calls for thorough thinking and discussion on both sides to ensure that conclusions are reached together.

The reason it was very easy for the second woman to back out after the first child had been killed and eaten is simple; she was thinking about herself! The reason five nations allied themselves against one, was simple; they wanted to put an end to the mystery of the power of the nation of Israel. They couldn't see beyond territories and treasures. The reason why the tower of Babel had to come down was simple; the people, even though they were able to harness the power of teams and collaboration, were not concerned for anything or anyone else but themselves.

Our God is not like that. He is the God who thrives on collaborations. Even though God the Father is all powerful, He joined with God the Son to bring about the redemptive plan and purpose for mankind. Despite the force of righteousness and purity with which God the Son walked the earth, He joined forces with God the Spirit to ensure that power is available and remains for His children to continue to live according to His design and pattern for us.

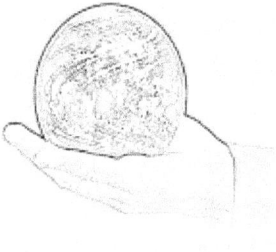

God always works for the good of mankind. Our destinies are always His utmost priority and He wants us all to come together and live out the mandate of righteousness, peace and joy in the Holy Ghost. What the world needs can only be found in God and not in a particular individual or group of persons. That is why we have to come

God always works for the good of mankind.

159

together, realign ourselves with God's purposes and begin to push His mandate for the Glory of His name.

We have to take a look again at how the things we chase after impact upon the Kingdom. We are all called to contribute our quota and a fresh understanding of what God wants to achieve is key to us aligning with His plan. The Apostle in the market place surely has his place. The Minister in charge of the flock has his place. The very wealthy man has his place. Even the not so wealthy has his place! There is a place for everyone within this mandate and the charge is simple, come and contribute your quota based on the resources God has put within you.

Sista Power Is About the Common Good

Let us pull down the walls and help to raise our children together. Let us mother without erecting walls. I want to know how I can add value to the children on the other side of the fence and I am open to receiving help from the other woman across the fence too. Let us stand together in prayer, rather than gossip about the challenges of the next person. This is a call to be intercessors for each other. We can stand together until that child returns home, we can stand together until healing comes to that body, we can stand together until the dignity of our men is restored, and we can stand together until our nation is rebuilt and values return to our society. We can stand as long as we remember that this is not about us receiving the recognition; we can stand as long as we understand that even when we are incognito God does know our labour and will reward us the way He deems fit. When we stand together to collaborate, we will bring about the required change and up-lifting of mankind together.

Let me sound a note of warning here. It will be foolhardy of us to think that without us, God cannot raise whomever He chooses to collaborate with in bringing about the change He desires. If you recall in chapter one I stated God's mandate for us in *Jeremiah 31:22b "... the Lord has begun a new thing, the woman will protect, intercede for, teach, nurture, love and care for humanity just as the father does."*

When those two women chose to conspire to eat their children, they failed in their responsibilities as mothers, protectors, intercessors teachers, nurturers and caregivers. They became selfish, monstrous and barbaric and I want to believe they were later punished for their heinous act.

However, in another place and time, God saw four people who were outcasts of the society; four lepers who decided to come together to collaborate. Their initial bottom line was of course selfish but when they saw that the blessings were more than they could handle they still came together in agreement, and brought the news of deliverance and victory to those in the city; even those who had cast them aside.[5]

God can use the downtrodden of the world to fulfill His divine mandate here on earth for the good of mankind. Therefore, as women, it is a great privilege and honour for God Almighty to place in our hands the destinies of many. He is expecting us to arise to the challenges, pull our resources together so we can win together just like the four lepers did and brought hope once gain to the famished land of Samaria in Israel.

At the beginning of 2011, I came in contact with an amazing woman of God. I saw her book, bought it, read it and realised that someone in the United States of America was living my life, just maybe five or seven years ahead of me. The more I thought about her, the more I could understand what my life was going to look like in a few years. As I made contact with Coach Anna McCoy, I had a hope in my heart that she would respond, and thank God she did. In that same year, she took the risk and left the comfort of her home and family to come and spend eight wonderful days with me and my family, friends and ministry in Nigeria, and the rest as they say is history. I can tell you categorically that my life is better because I came in contact with this woman and she made herself available to me. But more than that, more than a few women in Nigeria have been blessed by this connection and are still being blessed even as you read this. The collaboration began a long time before either of us knew the other existed. It began the day Coach Anna McCoy exercised the discipline to write the book Woman Act

Now. It continued the day I bought the book, read it and decided to make contact. And it continues till this day. Through this relationship, an expansion has come to her vision and an enlargement beyond words has come to mine. One thing that we both know and understand is that we are Midwives and therefore vessels to work out God's plan. For us it is not about the gain, it is about being where God has planted us. For this reason my daughter has a mother in the United States who remembers to pray for her when I may not be able to!

Through this relationship an expansion has come to her vision and an expansion beyond words has come to mine.

At some point in 2011 I had to undergo surgery, and in the two and half hours that I was out, Coach Anna led a team of women in the United States to stand in prayer for my life. My sisters in Lagos were standing in prayer too! Heaven was bombarded that day for my sake, but it was a day I could not pray. They held up my hands when I was weak! And that is what collaboration is all about. It is about stepping out with the assurance that someone else has my back. It is about being weak and recognising that someone will lend me their shoulder to lean on. It is about coming together to ensure that every good thing the Lord has promised the earth will be birthed through us.

So can we then redefine what our bottom line is? My bottom line is people. My bottom line is destinies. My bank account may not read many zeros as long as the bank of heaven records many souls. My collaboration is a success and it should be no different for you. No matter where you are and what you do, remember that it is God's plan that will stand, irrespective of what the plans of men are.

To define the bottom line in your collaborations, the following points should be given serious consideration.

- Let your core values be known. Discuss the things that are important to you, so that you can run with them and be on the same page.

- Ensure that the things that are important to you are things of the kingdom that will bless humanity and affect your generation, long after you are gone.

- Ensure that whatever things you decide to do should also be things that will add value to others. Do not be selfish.

Collaborative relationships should be respected whether it is convenient or not, especially when there are already laid down rules. That you are in collaboration does not give you the permission to invade the other person's space continuously. Let what concerns the other person concern you and be important to you. Identify your personal areas of strength and ensure that you give more to the relationship from your area of strength.

Action Exercise

i)   What is the difference between collaboration and conspiracy?

ii) Identify your areas of strength and capabilities that could be of advantage to your present and future collaborations.

iii) What, in your opinion, are the greatest impediments to collaboration for the greater good?

iv) How do you determine your bottom line when dealing with your co-collaborators?

8 THE MASTER'S BUSINESS REQUIRES URGENCY

As I write the last chapter of this book, it has taken me longer than I had thought to finish the book and I do know that I should have moved faster on this project than I had done. Why has it taken longer? Basically because I was distracted by other equally important things which is why I do recognise that sometimes we hear from God what to do but somehow, we don't move as quickly as He would have us move because life tends to happen and may derail us totally or take us off track momentarily. While the excuses are valid and make sense, whether they will be tenable before our King and Maker will be another matter altogether.

While the excuses are valid and make sense, whether they will be tenable before our King and Maker will be another matter altogether

The Foolish Virgins

In Matthew 25, we have Jesus telling His powerful parables, and in this particular chapter He tells first of the ten virgins; five foolish and five wise. They had heard that the bridegroom, to whose bridal train they belonged, was finally coming to town on a particular day and they had to go and meet with him and his party.

This was a special bridegroom and the circumstances were special too. The virgins quickly prepared themselves and took off for the venue of the wedding ceremony to wait for their bridegroom. Because they recognised that theirs was a special dispensation they took lamps just in case the bridegroom came at night, at least they would be ready with lights to brighten their pathway. And they waited and waited, finally, the bridegroom shows up late.

It was announced that the bridegroom was now ready for them and whomsoever had anything to do with the wedding needed to get inside the hall. Alas! Five of the virgins suddenly realised that their lamps were out of oil! They wanted their colleagues to give them some of the oil so they could make it in, but of course they could not share especially because they didn't know how long the ceremony was going to last! They had to run off to try and get more oil for their lamps and by the time they returned, it was too late. The doors had been shut and they were denied access into the ceremony that they had waited all their lives to attend.[1]

Someone had tried to argue with me a while ago that it was harsh what they did to the virgins. His argument was that they had trimmed their lamps and come, but had to use up their oil because the bridegroom took a long while coming. Like I mentioned earlier, the excuse will be valid but whether it is tenable will be another story all together. This encounter with the bridegroom was the reason the virgins were on earth, just the same way you and I are here to fulfill our destiny. Now because God is the author and finisher of our faith and because He works in a time frame and season entirely different from our own, our responsibility is to be ready at all times. The foolish virgins had a sense of their purpose, they just didn't prepare adequately for the moment!

The business of the Master requires haste. When the time comes for you to be the midwife that you have lived to be, it may take only a few minutes to make the impact that you are called to make, and after that the opportunity will be gone. To recognise your timing and to be adequately prepared and ready to walk in it, you as the midwife will have to be in tune with the Holy Spirit of God all the way. The virgins ran out of oil and oil is a symbol of the Holy Spirit. There was a disconnect between the virgins and their instructor so they didn't know the next logical step to take.

Now because God is the author and finisher of our faith and because He works in a time frame and season entirely different from our own, our responsibility is to be ready at all times.

Some people get upset when you say that God spoke to you, and they wonder if you are not showing off by saying that. But I have always wondered how you will survive in a world such as ours if you do not hear the instructions, admonitions and encouragement of your Master! Remember that collaborations are not about the individual gain and not about what an individual wants. Collaborations are about birthing destiny and bringing God's will to bear on earth! It is the reason every midwife needs a relationship with the Holy Spirit for herself.

An understanding and a knowing deep within your heart will enable you stay on course even when it seems the hardest thing to do! It is an ability to get information that no one has access to that will release the grace to make the required sacrifice so that the Master's business is attended to. Long time ago, I learnt that God works in seasons and in cycles. To get the best out of any season there is a need for me to recognise the season and work according to its dictates.

If, for instance, it is a season to sow, and I take out my sickle to go harvesting, the truth is I will return from the fields bearing nothing, because the action I had carried out within that period was the wrong one. However, if I recognise that it is the season for planting and I take my seeds and go to the field which I have prepared, then a few months down the road, I should be able to take my sickle out for a harvest.

Let us return to the daughters of Zelophehad for a minute, how come they picked that time to approach Moses to ask that they be given their inheritance? Who told them that the time was right? How on earth did they know that they will be granted their wish? I may not be able to tell you anything, but I am pretty sure that they had, if nothing else, a certain measure of peace in their hearts that this was the way to go.

Imagine for a minute that these five women decided to wait just a little longer, then Moses would have died and it would not have been right to saddle Joshua with such an awesome responsibility of altering the status quo right after his taking over the reins of control. Take a look and read all the issues that came up right after Joshua took over and you will see that a wish such as that of the daughters of Zelophehad would have been selfish and inconsiderate to say the least.

If Jochebed had delayed in placing Moses on the Nile or had Miriam delayed in approaching Pharoah's daughter, probably Moses would never have gotten the chance to be used by God to deliver the children of Israel

If Jochebed had delayed in placing Moses on the Nile or had Miriam delayed in approaching Pharoah's daughter, Moses probably would never have gotten the chance to be used by God to deliver the children of Israel. There must have been a divine peace these women experienced and a gentle nudging to make the move at the time they did. Now the truth is this, peace will not be void of an apprehension of how things will play out, but it doesn't in anyway negate the fact that the peace and assurance that this is what God will have you do is in your heart. Many times I have sensed God tell me what to do. Many times I have known for sure that it is what I should be doing, however, many times too I am afraid and scared of what the possible result will be but I go ahead anyway, because there is a peace that I have that keeps me going even though I am scared of what I will find.

Peter must have felt the same way too. When Jesus asked him to launch out into the deep, he was scared that nothing would happen just like it didn't all night. But nevertheless, he obeyed Jesus and caught a great multitude of fish. Ladies, the Master's business requires haste. In the same passage in Matthew 25, right after the parable of the wise and foolish virgins is another story that has stuck with me since the first time I heard it in Sunday school. This is the parable of the talents. We are told of three different servants, a master and the distribution of talents according to the ability possessed by each servant. The first one traded with what he got and doubled his investment; the second one did the exact same thing. The third one however had issues.

He was distracted by the fact that his master didn't seem to be a man whose business dealings were right and ethical. He probably didn't want to be told later that he had helped a man, whose business tactics he didn't understand, to gain more wealth so he buried his talent and gave it back the exact same way he had received it. The master was not thrilled to say the least. The talents had been given for change and for profit, but the third servant did none of the above and the Bible says it didn't sit well with the Master.[2]

For each one of us, there is an ability that has been given which if we utilize properly, has the potential to bring about change and create value for mankind. Now, sometimes we recognise this but we just think that surely God does not need that kind of ability. My question usually is, why then did He put it in you if He was not going to have a need for it?

Your Pulpit Is Where You Are

Rather than extend the invite to a formal church building, which may never be honoured, be the extension of God's hand right there.

Gone are the days when you needed a pulpit within the four walls of a Church building to be able to make divine impact. We have moved into the Apostolic Era, and wherever we are is our Pulpit! The lines of the divide are being progressively eroded. The veil has been torn and everyone is given the freeway. All God wants from us is to use what we have been given by Him, where we are, to bring about change and be midwives of destiny. Right there in the board room where you are, you can be a midwife! Rather than extend the invite to a formal church building, which may never be honoured, be the extension of God's hand right there. Model Christ and be there to give counsel that honours and empowers and you will be pushing your own pulpit!

The Master's business requires haste. We are running out of time. We need to begin to move and extend ourselves to ensure that our work receives the attention it requires. For everyone you have the opportunity of having in your life, recognise that they may not be in your life forever. Be ready to deposit in them whatever it is that you carry which they require so they can go on and pursue their destinies.

The Master's business requires haste, which means that it is no longer okay to sit down and do nothing about developing the abilities that we possess. There will never be a convenient time to do the work that God has called you to do. It is about making ourselves available and stretching ourselves for the sake of the Kingdom. The Master's business requires haste and that means we also have to choose wisely our midwives and submit ourselves to learn from them so we can go on and become midwives for others.

The charge is for us to recognise that we need to move and

we need to move now! Life is not going to wait and midwives are constantly on the move. God is in the business of adding value and collaboration is an active step in adding value.

At the end of the parable of the virgins, the five foolish virgins got oil and came back, but they were denied access into the ceremony venue. The person to whom you have access to midwife today may deny you access tomorrow! The day I reached out to Coach Anna McCoy, I had fear in my heart! It was not that she was physically with me or could harm me, but it was the fact that somehow, I struggle with the fear of rejection, and it does a lot of harm to me when I sense that I have been rejected. Everything looked like she was going to say no. There was nothing that indicated that she would be willing to connect with me at the level I was looking to connect. However, despite the fear and everything else that didn't seem to add up, there was the assurance that God wanted me to do this. I took the leap and jumped off the bridge that day, and it seemed that she had been waiting for me!

When God speaks to your heart, learn to listen and act. While this is not a book on how to hear God, it certainly is part of the responsibility of this book to encourage you to learn to hear God for yourself! I tell people that others are there to confirm to me what God has spoken to me, and anything short of that will be a misnomer.

A long time ago before I got married, I had an idea what kind of man God would have me marry. I was willing to wait, but I got in a group where the people liked to help God speed things along, so they told me God had told them that a particular person was my spouse. Now, nothing was wrong with this individual. But I knew that even though I didn't know who I was to marry yet, it was clear to me that he wasn't the person.

When I told them I was pretty sure he was not the one, they didn't take it well and that was the beginning of our separation. It was a huge blow to me at that time, because I thought surely these were meant to be my midwives. I took it in good faith and that separation was the reason I got moved into the neighbourhood where I eventually met my husband.

I had to be open, and even though I didn't like the move at the time, I went with it. Today every time I think about those days I thank God for what I learnt around those people and I praise God that they cast me out when they did.

The Master's business requires haste, and what this means is that we have to be careful and discerning not to miss our moment! You have got to hear God for yourself! No man should be the Holy Spirit to you

Jesus died to give you access and access is available to you to be able to reach the Father for yourself.

178

because no man has the license or authority to be a go-between between you and God. Jesus died to give you access and access is available to you to reach the Father for yourself.

The Master's business requires haste and that means you must also be able to submit yourself to process. The places God allows you to go, serve as midwives there to garner the experience that you require to become a superb midwife for others. Learn while you have the opportunity, and ensure that you learn well. A few years ago, a woman I respect greatly passed on to glory and it was a huge blow to ministry and to young people in my country! While people wept and mourned, I couldn't help thinking if we had all taken the advantage to learn all that we were meant to learn from her. While people wanted God to send her back, I couldn't help wondering if we learnt anything at all!

With the passing of time, when I come across those who were close to her and didn't learn anything, I remember that midwives are for a season, and if we learn well from them, then we will go on and be midwives for others.

The most important reason why this business requires haste however, is because we are running out of time! The Bible is quite clear on the fact that there is an end in sight and I shudder when I think even for a second that someone will not make it because I wasn't upholding my part of the bargain to create value and bring about change for them! Collaboration, as I have seen in teaching it over the past year, can also be quickly taken out of context and focused on personal gain, but it is not meant to be so. This is a call to further the business of the Master and whatever you give, give it with the Kingdom as the focus and as the goal.

As I close this book, I can see a better world where women stand for each other and do powerful things together for a great and powerful God because everyone brought their gift to the table and was humble enough to use it for the glory of God.

The world is waiting for you and me to exercise the dominion and authority that God has given us from the beginning of the world! There is a manifestation of the sons and daughters of God that all of creation eagerly awaits. It takes an understanding and a submission to the sovereign will of God to make this happen. And it will take women who are not afraid to step out and be the shoulders that others will stand on. Change is the objective, Kingdom is the goal, altering the status quo is the method. You carry something. I carry something. We all carry something and if we agree to bring it all together we will be able

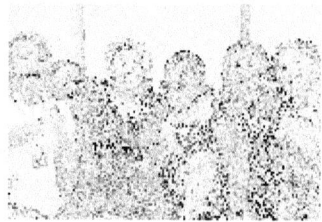

I can see a better world where women stand for each other and do powerful things together for a great and powerful God...

to invade our corner of the earth with heaven and God's kingdom.

We can do it because the Holy Spirit is waiting and willing to work it all out for us. Will you make yourself available? Will you make the required sacrifice, and will altering the status quo be the challenge you take on? I enlisted in the army for change when I realised that I could do something of value. I invite you to enlist too, and together let our little efforts make our God proud.

Thank you for taking the time to invest in this book, I speak the grace of collaboration over you and look forward to hearing that the principle worked for you. Arise my sisters because there is power inside of you!

God bless you!

Action Exercise

i) Do you know what your purpose is? What steps have you taken to walk in it?

ii) What are the next steps you should take in your life in order to follow on God's assignment for you?

iii) Identify the ways in which you have been slacking on the Master's business and ask for Grace to double up.

iv) Share your experience and what you have learnt with more Sistas. Encourage them to make the life changing decisions you have committed to.

EPILOGUE

AND A MOVEMENT BEGINS

When God spoke to me at the close of 2010, He gave me a word that birthed the writing of this book. In that time He has helped me forge and foster some awesome relationships; yet nothing could have prepared me for what the word COLLABORATION could have evolved to become.

This book was scheduled for release in July of 2012 to coincide with the year's edition of our conference Return of The Helper (ROTH). But despite everything that I did, we were unable to meet the target. If I had contracted another Publisher but my own company to publish it, I probably would have taken the work off their hands but alas, I was my own Publisher and yet could not deliver to myself.

It all started with my Coach Anna McCoy pointing out that something was missing from the book. I tried hard but couldn't ascertain what it was. Finally I resigned myself to the hands of Him who called me and gave me the mandate to write this book. I trusted that when He was ready things will move forward.

You know how the Bible in 1 Corinthians 13:9-10 says that we know in part and we prophesy in part, and that when perfection comes the imperfect disappears? Well, It turns out there is a new season that God wants to begin and He wanted me to add that the seed has been sown and is beginning to sprout.

Basically, it began the very next day after ROTH 2012, when we had the opportunity, my sistas and I, for the first time to all be in the same room with our spouses and witnesses. From the results of the conversations that we had it turns out that God was preparing us for a MOVEMENT all the while. The question is what is a Movement?

According to Social Movement exponent Marshall Ganz: Social movements emerge as a result of the efforts of purposeful actors (individuals, organizations) to assert new public values, form new relationships rooted in those values, and mobilize the political, economic, and cultural power to translate these values into action. They differ from fashions, styles, or fads (viral or otherwise) in that they are collective, strategic and organized. They differ from interest groups in that they focus less on allocating goods, than on redefining them; not only winning the game, but also changing the rules. Initiated in hopeful response to conditions adherents deem intolerable, social movement participants make moral claims based on renewed personal identities, collective identities, and public action.

In my layman's understanding, a movement is born when a group of people come together with the same focus and ideologies to push for change, which in the language of this book means altering the status quo.

Imagine when God, at that meeting and consequent ones, began to bring clarity to the word He had spoken so simply less than two years ago! What our collaborative efforts are meant to achieve is provide an enabling environment for women to dream, learn, launch and live their dreams! Women all over will come to our simple collaborations of threes or fours pushing the idea of a better life and a better society. In those pockets, with the consistency and momentum that result usually, a movement of women will be born. In our little group where we started individually as women trying to live the dreams of our hearts, we have seen how this can spark a movement beyond us.

Between Woman Act Now, Effectual Magazine and the Sistas, we have become an army of women spread across the continents, who come together daily to pull each other, hold each other accountable, pray for each other and love each other enough to contend that the highest possible good be made manifest concerning us. In the few months that I have lived this mandate and pushed it, it has become clear to me that somehow, my life, connected to all the other women in my space is richer and better.

The collaborative efforts of seven women have now grown beyond us and have begun to rub off on our spouses, children and even extended families. Friends of our collaborators have become our friends by extension and the idea that it is possible for women to be supportive of each other, to fulfill destinies and bring change is fast catching on. These efforts are beginning to spin off circles of their own and it is clear that out of this one word, greatness has begun to emerge. I now have families in the United States looking out for my good.

This movement is spilling over into affecting not just our immediate environments but even the stories of our nations and how generations have lived in the knowledge of single stories. From just two women making a connection great things are happening to move the story of collaboration to different circles of influence. This summer alone, my Coach had thirteen Nigerians in her home over a period of one week and it was family all the way. Who could have known how one effort can spin off to so many branches? And it is still spinning! Our children are finding that when they travel across borders to pursue an education, this collaboration is waiting with its gains! Who knew?

By this epilogue, I am setting the tone for the future so that you, the reader, will be able to identify where your collective power can take you. This is not about us, it is about destiny, and it is about our families. It is about the fact that other women will come learn how you did it because it is what they require to grow too.

Sistapower is therefore not a book about how women will take over, instead it is about how women can come together to resolve conflicts, tell stories, birth hope and nurture change in our world. Truly in the words of Jeremiah 31:22 …the Lord has begun a new thing; a woman shall encompass the world!

Join us! Let the MOVEMENT of love and change begin!

BONUS READ

Selected Articles from the Sistapower column of
Effectual Magazine, written by the author.

Effectual Magazine, a bi-monthly magazine is the flagship publication of Verbatim Communications. Since its maiden edition in 2004, It has continued to be a source of inspiration and practical resource for empowered living for women and those who love them.

IT TAKES A VILLAGE

Growing up, I had issues, and as a teenager it seemed like my issues were going to be the end of me. At the root of it all was low self esteem, but it manifested as rebellion. It wasn't because I grew up in an abusive environment, even though that was part of it, but it was just the way I was wired.

My parents wanted the very best for me, and my mother would do her best to ensure that I didn't stray too far away. Her solution? She put me on an extremely short leash, but short as that leash was, I always found a way to get away and into all kinds of trouble. The unfortunate thing then was I never got into trouble I could handle by myself, it was usually beyond me and so my mother always had to step in. As a parent you will recognize that this can be a very frustrating experience, and so it was for my parents, especially for my mother.

At this time my mother had a friend, she wasn't related to us in anyway but she was a friend indeed. When I would step out of the zone and get in trouble and my mother would be engaging in the tired mode, she would take over. Every time she took over from my mother, I found out that it was easier to bear. It wasn't that she didn't tell me the truth but maybe because I wasn't her biological daughter she could be a lot more objective, and that environment gave me the opportunity to thrive.

The reason I am narrating this ordeal in my mother's life is because the expression 'it takes a village' was just apt for my situation. As women we are led more by our emotions than by objectivity or reason. It certainly couldn't be easy for a mother to watch her child get on the path of destruction without looking back. The fear that one will end up a bad mother is there and of course there is no mentioning the trepidation of looking like a failure among the motherhood category. So my mother sometimes panicked, and lashed out in frustration at other times. But my aunty? She was always calm and she could reach me when no one else could.

Sista power is about collaborations; where one woman stands in the gap for the other woman to ensure that she succeeds. It is a 'She wins you Win' scenario. Do whatever you can to contribute to her success and when it's your turn she will do exactly the same.

Every time she took over from my mother, I found out that it was easier to bear.

190

Those days growing up, women did this for each other. Mothers had friends to whom they sent their children when the issue was too tricky or sensitive.

To make impact, therefore, I am thinking that as a mother, I will deliberately get into relationships with women, who can influence my children positively, especially in ways I may not be equipped to do. It takes a village to raise a child and rather than hide what is up with your children, look for someone who may be able to make a difference and build a bridge to reach them.

It worked for me! As I tell this story my mother and aunty are still friends, some thirty years later; and every time I think of her, I am grateful she was the one my mother chose as her friend at that point in my life. Who are your friends? Can you entrust your children to them? Will they do right by them?

Remember, motherhood is a tough job, and whatever anyone can chip in to ensure your success will be an advantage... so enlist the help of your (trustworthy, God fearing and honest) friends because your child may just be one of those counting on the village to raise him/her.

God bless and empower you.

BONUS READ

THE SISTERHOOD

*A*s the year came to a close I felt an impression in my heart, put there by God, that in the New Year, I personally had need to network more with women. It was pretty much the fact that some of the things I was looking for, some women already had and were looking for somewhere to pour into.

So I prayed and I am still praying real hard for God to bring into my life the right kind of women, who have the same heart after God that I am trying to develop.

So I entered 2011, with the mindset to deliberately pick and nurture my relationships with other women on a scope wider than I had done all my life. To be able to do this I had to deal with the fear that women never look after their own. I had to deal with the phobia that women are always looking for other women to pull down. So I prayed and I am still praying real hard for

God to bring into my life the right kind of women, who have the same heart after God that I am trying to develop.

I am sure you want to know how I have fared; it has been a great experience. One thing is clear to me now, and it is the fact that there are other women all over the world who have the same yearning in my heart and I know God will continue to bring me in contact with them to make powerful connections for the sake of womanhood and humanity.

Two other events made it imperative that I speak about this yearning on this page. The first was about the shootings in Arizona where so many people were killed and injured, including a female US Rep. Gabrielle Giffords. We have all watched and hoped and prayed that she gets back on her feet. But then today I stumbled on an article someone had sent to me, on the fact that when she opened her eyes for the first time in the hospital, she had her family members and… wait for it, her female co-workers and friends around her.

This resonated so much in my spirit and I wondered if there will be any women willing to do vigil at my bedside had it happened to me. I also had to quickly ask myself, "Is there a woman for whom I will vigil?"

The second event was the PDP Presidential primaries here in Nigeria, and how for the first time, a woman Mrs. Sarah

Jubril made it to the primaries. Yes, she had only one vote, but I looked at the pictures and I didn't see any woman standing by her, cheering her on. No wonder all she got was one vote! She was such a lone voice in the wilderness. Now this is not about qualifications, this is about being there for one another!

The next time we have a female presidential candidate, or any candidate for that matter, remember that we need to stand together.

When Mary found out she was pregnant, and didn't fully understand what was going on, she sought out one of her own; Elizabeth, and for six months they lived together and I have a feeling Mary must have felt better. When Naomi's life hit the roughest patch ever, she had Ruth. The rest is history.

While it is great to have a powerful marital relationship that has your back, I think it is about time we started to forge powerful relationships amongst the womenfolk. Let's go back to how they did it in bible days, when they stood for and with each other. Let us return to the days of our mothers, when every woman on the block had a say about how the children were raised. Whether she had children of her own or not! Let us go back to the days when the women would agree and stand in the place of agreement until they obtain results. Where did the women go?

To the women in my life, I wish I could mention all your names, I want to say thank you. Because today, I recognize that your place in my life is powerful. Thank you Kate, Sarah, Audrey, Shade, Sola, Enife, Tayo, Evelyn, Charity, Nkiruka, Oghogho, Tonia, Isioma, Victoria, Ngozi, Seyi, Inyang, Patience, Anna... I wish I could mention all your names, thank you and God bless you.

Now it is your turn, who are the women in your life? What are your relationships like? Make powerful connections this year, because there is a unique power available when Sistas connect.

MY LOVE FOR INI AND SHOES

Sometime ago I wrote about my bag 'fetish.' Maybe it is time to make another confession, and it is ...hmmm... my love for shoes! I love shoes and I love shoes, oh yes shoes are my thing. But that was until I met Ini. She is my sister and even though we were not born of the same parents, we are sisters all the same. Ini is not just someone I met on the streets of Lagos, she is a woman I admire and look up to. She is strong, just like I want to be. She is bold as I hope to be sometime. She is nice as I aspire to be, (she can be mean just as I am sometimes.) But above all, Ini dares to dream!

More than all these attributes though, there is something else we have in common and it is our love for shoes! I have seen Ini's collection of shoes and boy, did I salivate the first time I saw them! And so no matter what happens, we will always find something to talk about; we will talk about shoes. It is not hard to find something to fight about either, we can fight about shoes.

However, this shoe tie goes beyond just shoes. We cry together, we can be scared together and we will always dream together. She says to me, 'I want to achieve this,' and I say to her, 'go on Sis, I've got your back.' When she is afraid she says, 'I cannot go on,' and I say 'Sis, yes you can.' I also do know that we will win together, and that is because she is my sister. When I am afraid, I can run to her too, and when I mess up, I am not afraid she will judge me.

Like my connection with Ini, every connection should have something other than the very serious and hard stuff. So between Ini and me we have got shoes. When the subject is difficult to broach we begin with the shoes, when it is too painful to continue, we can always switch to the shoes.

What has happened between me and Ini is that we have found common ground, and this ground is solid enough for us to begin to build whatever we want to build. Sometimes I sit and think, 'What if we no longer have feet for shoes?' And then I say, 'We will together look for those who have feet and we will love shoes on their behalf!' Sisters, my point is this, for the sisterhood to make impact, there must be something that

However, this shoe tie goes beyond just shoes. We cry together, we can be scared together and we will always dream together

198

serves as common ground. Agreed, what I have with Ini seems very unimportant, but that is okay for us because it works! You just need to find your own common ground. Maybe it is a cause, maybe it is a dream, but we have found that when the cause overwhelms and when the dream becomes hard to push, we can always come back to the shoes.

This is the story of my love for Ini and shoes; I do hope you have a story to tell too. At least you can tell that I am connecting and I am pushing with this one woman. Till next edition when I bring you another Sista in whom I am well pleased, remember the trick is to find something none of you will tire of too soon.

Sistas, yes we can!

SHONNA: THE ARMOUR BEARER

During the week of Return of the Helper (our annual conference) I found out that sistahood is not limited by borders or continents. I had two wonderful sisters in from the United States, Coach Anna McCoy and Shonna Stallworth.

Leading up to their arrival in Nigeria, I had no way of knowing what to expect. I wasn't sure how they expected me to act around them; I was becoming flustered so I decided that rather than be confused or desperate I was just going to be myself and hopefully they will see the authentic me through it all. Of course with her wonderful charm and grace, Coach helped me though the first meeting jitters and before I knew what was happening we were chatting away like I had known them all my life.

They were very gracious guests, didn't put anything on us that we couldn't afford nor did they make any demands that were out of the ordinary. (I am really grateful Sistas)

Now Shonna! From the moment I met her at the airport I realized that she was both tough and soft at the same time. She was going to give us whatever we deserved depending on how we engaged. And she did a marvelous job of being like that through their stay. Thankfully, we never really got to see her tough side, because I believe God's grace covered us!

What stood out for me through their stay though was how she ensured that Coach had the best of everything. She could just anticipate her need even before she spoke a word. I realized that even with Coach, she could be respectfully firm because like she said to me 'I am her armour bearer.'

Shonna had been in Coach Anna's life for eight years, and you could see that these two shared a love that was real and genuine yet each one knew her place and filled it without any kind of attitude except that of love. Shonna was very willing to stay in the background as long as she was sure that Coach was safe and was living her destiny. I saw a young woman who had no ambition on that trip but to ensure that Coach had the best time.

It was no wonder to me then, that at every turn, Coach took the opportunity to celebrate her too.

From the moment I met her at the airport I realized that she was both tough and soft at the same

Watching them relate, I had to ask myself how easy it is for someone equally talented and gifted to stay in the background just to let another shine because they are sisters? I realized that Shonna's day will come, and I prayed a short prayer that day that she will find her own armour bearer who will not be intimidated by her strength.

I had to ask myself, will I be willing to stay in the background for anyone? Then I realized, isn't that what all of this Sista power thing is about? Yes I will humbly stay in the background for my sistas because I recognize that it is no competition and everyone will have their day, (God helping me that is!)

Ladies, who will you be an armour bearer for? Who will you pour of yourself into the way Shonna gave and still gives of herself to Coach? Are we willing to put our agenda aside so we can really serve another's dream?

The truth of the matter is that after all is said and done, all we have to offer each other is ourselves, because ideas come a dime a dozen. The best thing I can give you is of myself, the best thing you can give me, more than money and gifts will be to put yourself at my disposal. Often we hear that women cannot be there for each other, but I think we can start our own revolution; we can begin to identify whose armour we will each carry, and when they make it into destiny you will be amazed that others will carry your armour too.

Shonna, from all your sisters here in Nigeria; thank you for making life easy for Coach Anna so she can go round the world and help others like us grow. You are loved and appreciated!

REMI: GPS SISTA

Welcome, to God moments and momentous people. Trust you enjoyed reading and were blessed by the piece on Shonna Stallworth as I enjoyed writing it.

Every time people write in or call to express how much they have been blessed by Effectual, they usually will direct their comments to me. And for that I am immensely grateful. However, I wish I can really take all the credit for this work, but I cannot and do not intend to. Effectual is powered by a team of people, some who are still here and some who have moved on to other dreams.

On Sista Power, we celebrate Sistas who empower other Sistas and point out how peculiarly they have added value to their unique relationship. So on this edition; I am celebrating my Sista and Managing Editor, Remi Oyeyemi for her dedication and commitment to my dream.

When you come across Remi for the first time, your first impression will be (at least that was mine), how frail and gentle she looks! For someone who knows me well enough, you will probably wonder if she will survive the hurricane that I am! But Remi has so much power packed into her that her frame and disposition is actually some façade that I am yet to understand what God is set to achieve with.

Remi makes it easy for me to breathe and dream. Because I am some kind of professional dreamer, whenever I come to her to say I think we should be doing so and so, and will she please find out for me what the process will be? Even though I can see that she is visibly at a loss for what I am talking about, she always, always responds "Okay Sistar B" and maybe days later, Remi comes to me with a process and today I want to say thank you.

Now some people may think it is because Remi is, in a manner of speaking, working for me that she plugs in so easily but I beg to disagree. Remi plugs in because she is just as interested in my dreams and vision succeeding as I am. When I look at her I do not see a member of staff, I see a co-labourer in a vineyard that, it is my hope, will bring the reward that she is looking for in life!

Remi has so much power packed into her that her frame and disposition is actually some facade that I am yet to understand what God is set to achieve with.

The question now will be if she is not a member of staff, what then is she? Well the power that she brings into this dream is for me the power of clarity. I have a knack for dreaming and seeing the end product; Remi helps me set and put together the processes, bringing clarity to all that I dream of achieving.

I have learnt from Remi that you do not have to have physical energy and stamina but if you are willing to contribute your quota from your own strength zone, you can bring very great value to the relationship. I can see a young woman very confident in her capacity and willing to share of herself even when credit goes elsewhere. What I have learnt and you can learn from Remi is that all you need to add value in your relationship, is all that you are, no more, no less. From your core, you can do things people stronger and smarter may not be able to do, because your heart is in it.

What I have also learnt from Remi, is the fact that she never takes on a task that is not from her strength zone, just as she is always willing to stretch herself as long as she is able to find even a jot of the ability in her. It is this 'realness' that I enjoy most in our relationship. There is also the trust principle, I am confident she will be standing at the post, even if I am not. Looking at her quiet strength makes me want to win. To tell you the truth, every sista needs a sista like her. One who will quietly wait with you to ensure that you birth a live baby, one who is willing to allow you lean on her where you may not be very strong.

Even the best and strongest of us require a shoulder. To find that sista may be difficult, but with Remi I have learnt that she doesn't have to be exactly like you, as long as she brings something and is willing to share it at the table. Just knowing she will ride with you even in stormy weather is the comfort that your relationship needs and should have.

I use this opportunity to say to Remi, my little sister, my friend and co-labourer that I appreciate you and you have taught me many things even though you know it not. My prayer is that your own dreams will all manifest and your own co-labourers and mid wives will show up in your moment. But above all, I pray that I will be able to be to you, half the Sista you have been to me and my dream.

You are loved and appreciated.

Bidemi

NOTES

Chapter 1

1. Mary jean pigeon, woman: purpose, position and power. destiny image publishers, 1998
2. Leviticus 26:8

Chapter 3

1. http://www.essentiallifeskills.net/personalvalue system.html
2. http://www.briannorris.com/passion/what-is-passion.html
3. http://jerry-lopper.suite101.com/what-is-belief--a5578
4. http://www.cdtl.nus.edu.sg/success/sl20.htm

Chapter 4

1. Gen 11:6-7

Chapter 5

1. http://thequestrevealed.com/success-in-internet-marketing-and-joe-girards-law-of-250/
2. John Maxwell, The 21 Irrefutable Laws of Leadership, (Thomas Nelson, 1998 and 2007)
3. http://www.azcharacteredfoundation.org/character.html

Chapter 6

1. Judges 4:4-21

Chapter 7

1. 2 Kings 6: 25-29.
2. Psalm 15:4
3. 1 chronicles 16:22
4. 1 Peter 2:9-10
5. 2 kings7:3-10

Chapter 8

1. Matthew 25:1-13
2. Matthew 25:14-30

IMAGES

Chapter 1

1. www.ebibleteacher.com
2. http://www.freeclipartnow.com/people/children/child-planting.jpg.html
3. http://www.housinghope.org/whatsNew/StoneSoup.html
4.http://www.freeclipartnow.com/construction/tools/gardening/fence.jpg.html
5. www.ciker.com
6. interactivity.ifactory.com

Chapter 2

1. www.powsley.blogspot.com
2. http://www.freeclipartnow.com/recreation/dancing/dancing-couple.jpg.html
3. www.misskiekabainie.blogspot.com
4. http://www.bibleexplained.com/moses/Exod/ex02.html
5. zambia.primaryblogger.co.uk
6. www.jw.org

Chapter 3
1. www.creativitypost.com
2. http://www.free-clipart-pictures.net/praying_hands_clipart.html
3. http://www.how-to-draw-cartoons-online.com/cartoon-angel.html
4. http://www.clipartof.com/portfolio/toonaday/open-door
5. http://www.cartoonstock.com/directory/v/virgin_birth.asp
6. josie.maudlinmayhem.com
7. www.solopreneur-blueprint.com

Chapter 4
1. www.pureclipart.com
2. www.screwattack.com
3. www.godsoutreachministryint.org
4. www.clarkewoodconsulting.blogspot.com
5. www.huwaaron.com
6. www.hem-of-his-garment-bible-study.org
7. www.askgramps.org
8. http://shaenon.livejournal.com/15446.html

Chapter 5
1. http://www.wpclipart.com/tools/index.html
2. www.vectorstock.com
3. http://www.nist.gov/pml/wmd/metric/trade-comm.cfm
4. http://etc.usf.edu/clipart/
5. www.kidsbiblestoriess.blogspot.com
6. www.urbanbellemag.com
7. www.workshopsbywoodard.com
8. www.elev8.com

Chapter 6

1. www.iconarchive.com
2. http://all-free-download.com/free-vector/vector-icon
3. http://all-free-download.com/comic_characters_painter_clip_art_25037.html
4. http://all-free-download.com/teenager_illustrations_58480.html

Chapter 7

1. http://all-free-download.com/bulle_gauche_stop_clip_art_22928.html
2. http://colleen-colleensblogblogspotcom.blogspot.com/
3. odt.co.nz
4. http://all-free-download.com/crawling_soldier_clip_art_23409.html
5. http://www.oneyearbibleblog.com/2012/06/june-9th-one-year-bible-readings.html
6. www.theprospectorsite.com
7. www.soundanalarm.com

Chapter 8

1. www.declamorous.blogspot.com
2. http://fredericksburgchurchofchrist.com/nt-coloring-book.htm
3. http://all-free-download.com/free-vector/vector-clip-art/
4. http://teachkidsaboutchrist.com/old-testament/baby-moses-coloring-page
5. http://all-free-download.com/free-vector/vector-clip-art/
6. http://dailycoloringpages.com/images/jesus-on-cross-coloring-pages-05.png

IMAGES

www.freestockphotos.biz
www.free-clipart-pictures.net/praying_hands_clipart.html
www.clipartof.com

SISTAPOWER